PHASE:

A TIMEFRAME

IN A KID'S LIFE WHEN YOU CAN

LEVERAGE

DISTINCTIVE | OPPORTUNITIES | TO | INFLUENCE

THEIR **FUTURE.**

ZERO
TO ONE

THE PHASE WHEN NOBODY SLEEPS,
EVERYBODY SMELLS, AND ONE
MESMERIZING BABY CONVINCES
YOU, "I NEED YOU NOW."

YOU HAVE APPROXIMATELY
936 WEEKS FROM THE
TIME YOUR CHILD IS BORN
UNTIL THE DAY THEY
GRADUATE AND MOVE TO
WHAT'S NEXT.

"TEACH US TO NUMBER OUR DAYS
(OR MAYBE WEEKS)
THAT WE MAY GAIN A HEART OF WISDOM."

PSALM 90:12

ZERO TO ONE
PARENTING THROUGH THE "I NEED YOU" PHASE

www.JustaPhase.com
Published by Orange, a division of The reThink Group, Inc.,
5870 Charlotte Lane, Suite 300,
Cumming, GA 30040 U.S.A.

Scripture quotations marked NLT are taken from the Holy Bible, New Living
Translation, Copyright 1996. Used by permission of Tyndale House Publishers, Inc., Wheaton, Illinois 60189.

All other Scripture quotations, unless otherwise noted, are taken from the
Holy Bible, New International Version®. NIV®. Copyright © 1973, 1978,
1984 by International Bible Society. Used by permission of Zondervan.
Other Orange products are available online and direct from the publisher.
Visit our website at www.ThinkOrange.com for more resources like these.

ISBN: 978-1-941259-42-9

©2015 Reggie Joiner and Kristen Ivy
Authors: Reggie Joiner and Kristen Ivy
Lead Editor: Karen Wilson
Editing Team: Mike Jeffries and Natalie White

Art Direction: Ryan Boon and Hudson Phillips

Book Design: FiveStone
Printed in the United States of America
First Edition 2015
1 2 3 4 5 6 7 8 9 10

ZERO
TO ONE

PARENTING THROUGH THE
"I NEED YOU NOW" PHASE

REGGIE JOINER & KRISTEN IVY

ENDORSEMENTS

"Parents who are trying to decide if they have what it takes will find encouragement, humor, and expertise in these pages from Kristen Ivy and Reggie Joiner. With practical advice for parents at any experience level, this guide to the Zero to One phase will make life a little easier and make the big picture a lot brighter."

SHERRY SURRATT, CEO, MOPS INTERNATIONAL

"Not only is the *It's Just A Phase* series of books the most creative and well thought out guide to parenting I have ever encountered, these books are ESSENTIAL to my DAILY parenting. With a 13-year-old, 11-year-old, and 9-year-old at home, I am swimming in their wake of daily drama and delicacy. These books are a reminder to enjoy every second. Because it's Just A Phase."

CARLOS WHITTAKER, AUTHOR AND SPEAKER

"There's nothing more precious than a newborn baby, but as a parent you might soon begin to wonder what you have gotten yourself into. Reggie and Kristen not only show us what to expect during the first year of a baby's life, but they give us some everyday ideas so we don't miss the magic of a single moment. This is the beginning of something wonderful!"

SUE MILLER, SPEAKER AND CHILDREN'S MINISTRY CONSULTANT

"We all know where we want to end up in our parenting, but how to get there can seem like an unsolved mystery. Through the *It's Just a Phase* series, Reggie Joiner and Kristin Ivy team up to help us out. The result is a resource that guides us through the different seasons of raising children, and provides a road map to parenting in such a way that we finish up with very few regrets."

SANDRA STANLEY, FOSTER CARE ADVOCATE, BLOGGER, WIFE TO ANDY STANLEY, AND MOTHER OF THREE.

TABLE OF CONTENTS

THERE IS NOTHING LIKE SLEEP DEPRIVATION IN THE HOME OF NEW PARENTS.

Maybe that's why every book on babies seems to be primarily dedicated to keeping them happy (stop the crying, please!) or helping them sleep longer (so parents can sleep longer). Sleep is the most-prized commodity of parents at this phase. In fact, if you're the stop-by-the-home-of-new-parents type just remember this: a sleeping baby is your cue not to stay.

IF YOU WONDER WHY EVERYBODY SMELLS, CONSIDER THIS:

When faced with the choice between sleep or a shower, there are days (no one's counting how many) when cleanliness doesn't win out. That's not to mention the dirty diapers or spit-up. The smells aren't all bad though. Just watch how long it takes grandma to lean over and sniff a new baby the first time she meets him.

THE GREATEST CHARACTERISTIC OF THIS PHASE BY FAR IS JUST HOW MUCH A BABY NEEDS YOU.

They need you more desperately, more consistently, and more frequently than at any other stage of life. They need you to feed them. They need you to clean up their messes. They need you to help them get to sleep. They need you to comfort them. They need you to smile at them, entertain them, and engage them. They're completely dependent on you in a way they never will be again. There is remarkable potential in the life of a new baby. And although the days are long, and the task can feel demanding, only one thing matters most at this phase: You show up.

IT'S JUST
A PHASE

SO DON'T
MISS IT

ZERO TO ONE
THE BEST PHASE

BY HOLLY CRAWSHAW

Regardless of how many friends, family members, and perfect strangers strive to paint an accurate picture of parenthood, there's really nothing anyone can say that adequately prepares you for that heart-stretching moment when you hold your newborn for the very first time.

And the sentiments only grow exponentially from there. There aren't words in any language capable of conveying the myriad of emotions you will experience as a new parent. Love. Gratitude. Exhaustion. Fear. Joy. Frustration. Excitement. Hate.

(Okay, you won't *really* hate your baby, but you likely will hate the sound of your baby crying at three in the morning when it's only been half an hour since his last feeding.)

Maybe that's the best word to describe the zero to one phase: *Emotional.* It's emotional for you. It's emotional for them. But despite the crying— both theirs and yours—there is something indescribably wonderful about that first year of life.

Somewhere along the way, in the delirium of teething, and feedings, and diapers, and sleep schedules, something almost magical takes place.

It's in the way your baby smells after a bath, wrapped in a towel and laying on your chest. It's in the way their eyelids flutter when they sleep. It's in the shape of their perfect little mouths, the length of their tiny fingernails, and the velvety feel of their skin against yours. There's something alluring about the way they are totally and completely brand new.

In my work as a preschool director, my favorite rooms to visit were the ones assigned to the zero to one age group. These were my volunteers'

favorite rooms, too. People literally wait in line to hold a baby. To rock a baby. To ooooh and ahhhh over a baby's impossibly long eyelashes or new hairbow.

There is a great sense of promise that adds to this age. Literally, anything is possible. The pages of their story are gleamingly blank, striking with potential.

As a parent, you have many phases ahead, and each one has its own set of unique possibilities. But right here, right now, you have something you will never have again—at least not in this way. You could think about it like this: You will never have messed up less as a parent than you have at this moment. Really. This is the beginning. You have a fresh start. This brand new life is in your hands. And even though it's scary, even though you don't know what you're doing (none of us ever do), you have everything your baby needs.

That's right. Because despite the thousands of mass-market baby products available, there is only one thing your baby really needs right now—your baby needs you.

Some days it may seem like they need you a little too much, or a little too often, or a little too immediately. Don't worry. With every passing month, they will discover a new ability that lets them need you a little less.

But for now, in this fleeting zero to one phase, they need you. And you are enough.

Holly Crawshaw
Preschool Director, Educator & Author

EVERY BABY

ZERO TO ONE

SOME MAY SLEEP THROUGH THE NIGHT AT SIX WEEKS OLD.

SOME DON'T SLEEP THROUGH THE NIGHT FOR ANOTHER SIX YEARS.

SOME MAY CRY WHEN YOU PUT THEM IN THEIR CAR SEAT.

SOME CRY UNLESS YOU PUT THEM IN THEIR CAR SEAT.

SOME START WALKING BY THE TIME THEY ARE SEVEN MONTHS OLD.

SOME THINK ABOUT TRYING TO ROLL OVER BY THE TIME THEY ARE SEVEN MONTHS OLD.

SOME WANT TO SUCK ON A PACIFIER.

SOME WANT TO SUCK THEIR THUMB.

SOME WANT TO SUCK ON EVERYTHING.

→ # IS UNIQUE

SOME WILL POOP
ONCE A DAY.

SOME WILL POOP
TEN TIMES A DAY.

SOME WILL LOOK JUST LIKE
AUNT CONNIE.

SOME WILL LOOK LIKE NO ONE YOU
HAVE EVER SEEN BEFORE.

SOME BABIES MIGHT SWIM
THE LENGTH OF A 25 METER
POOL BY NINE MONTHS
(YOURS PROBABLY WON'T).

EVEN WITH UNIQUE BABIES—WHICH YOURS MOST CERTAINLY IS—
MOST BABIES **ZERO TO ONE** HAVE A FEW THINGS IN COMMON.
THIS BOOK WILL SHOW YOU WHAT THOSE ARE SO YOU CAN MAKE
THE MOST OF THE "I NEED YOU NOW" PHASE WITH YOUR BABY.

REMEMBER:
WE HAVEN'T MET YOUR BABY.

THIS BOOK IS
JUST ABOUT A
LOT OF BABIES.

FOR
SOME

ZERO
TO
ONE

THINGS YOU MIGHT SAY AS A NEW PARENT

DO I SMELL LIKE BABY VOMIT?

ARE THEY ASLEEP YET?

DID I EAT TODAY?

NO ONE TOLD ME THAT.

WHEN WAS MY LAST SHOWER?

SHOULD I
NAP
OR SHOULD I
SHOWER?

DO NOT
RING THE DOORBELL.
↓
BABY SLEEPING.

SOUNDS LIKE

YOU'VE PROBABLY NEVER SAID BEFORE . . .

WHEN IS YOUR MOM COMING?

WHEN IS YOUR MOM LEAVING?

SHHH, SHHH, SHHH, SHHH,

SHHH

PLEASE PLEASE PLEASE PLEASE DON'T CRY RIGHT HERE

HEY.

HEY. HEY. DON'T FALL ASLEEP YET.

THAT'S THE MOST BEAUTIFUL FACE I'VE EVER SEEN.

IT'S YOUR TURN.

I'M JUST GOING TO DRIVE AROUND THE NEIGHBORHOOD FOR ANOTHER HOUR.

DID I GET ANYTHING DONE TODAY?

YOU HAVE TO COVER THAT UP WHEN YOU CHANGE THE DIAPER.

WHY.ARE.YOU.CRYING?

UNDER

THE SIX WAYS YOUR

PHYSICALLY  **1**

MENTALLY **2**

CULTURALLY **3**

STAND

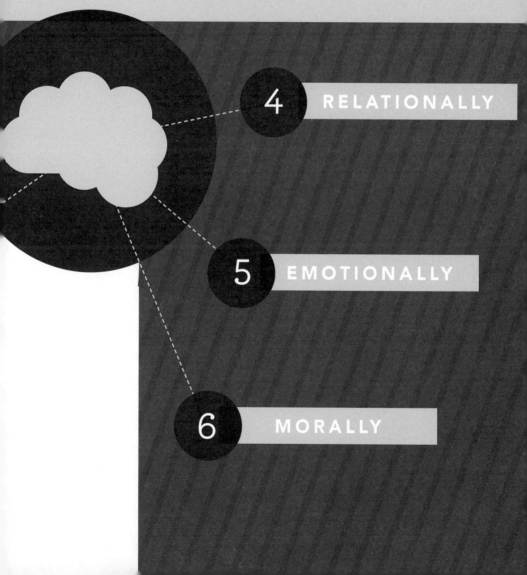

→ **BABY IS CHANGING**

4 RELATIONALLY

5 EMOTIONALLY

6 MORALLY

You have approximately 936 weeks from the time your child is born until the day they graduate and move to what's next.

The weeks won't look the same.
Your child is constantly changing.
They will go through many phases.
And every phase will be unique.

As a parent, one of your roles is to rediscover your child in each phase—
to pay attention to the changes.
to notice the shifts.
to understand what is new.

WEEKS

This section won't solve your most pressing parenting questions—like how to get your newborn to sleep. Instead, this section is designed to introduce you to your child in a new way.

At every phase, your child is changing in six ways. By exploring those changes, we hope you will be even more fascinated by who they are and how they perceive the world.

SO DON'T MISS
THE PRESENT
REALITIES OF ...

ZERO
TO
ONE

one

WHAT'S CHANGING PHYSICALLY

One of the most distinctive attributes of the zero to one phase is how quickly babies change. At a few days old, most kids look like someone's angry great-uncle. Then, by their first birthday, a walking, babbling creature with a head full of teeth emerges, and you may be able to pick out Dad's nose or Mom's ears.

While it may seem like these changes happen overnight, they are actually happening week by week, month by month, season by season.

THEIR SIZE IS CHANGING

Whether your baby was born in the 10th percentile or the 85th, one thing is true: they are growing—fast. The average baby doubles his birth weight by the time he is four months old and triples his birth weight by his first birthday. Imagine if you were still growing at that same pace!

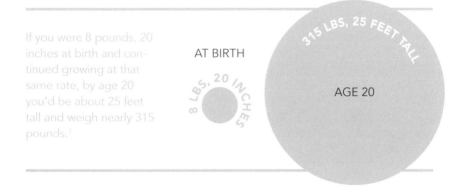

If you were 8 pounds, 20 inches at birth and continued growing at that same rate, by age 20 you'd be about 25 feet tall and weigh nearly 315 pounds.[1]

AT BIRTH

8 LBS, 20 INCHES

315 LBS, 25 FEET TALL

AGE 20

If you ever find yourself getting anxious about your little's one's growth—whether it seems like too much or too little—remember that's what pediatricians are for. You can also follow along in those in-between-check-up times by looking at growth charts from the World Health Organization.[2]

THEIR SENSES ARE CHANGING

Your baby was born with fully functioning ears that know and prefer the sound of your voice.[3] Their vision isn't quite so developed. But, from zero to one, your baby's eyesight will develop significantly.

At birth, your baby's vision is roughly 20/200-20/400 and two-dimensional. This means they see objects best when they are a foot away—the perfect distance to focus on the person holding them.

Even with their changing vision, babies prefer to look at . . .
» high contrast objects (black and white) over subtle colors.[4]
» people over objects (particularly faces).[5]
» faces who make eye contact over those who don't.[6]
» their parents' faces over anyone else (even at only 12-36 hours old).[7]

By eight months, your baby's vision (and eye color) will almost be fully developed. At the end of this phase, your baby will literally be seeing the world in a whole new way.

THEIR MOVEMENTS ARE CHANGING

Your baby's changes in mobility are like a precursor to their SAT score. Everyone asks about it. Relatives talk about it. Parents worry about it. Whether your baby is an early crawler, a late crawler, or not a crawler, allow yourself to be fascinated by the progress your baby makes in these twelve months.

Generally speaking, your baby will accomplish a lot from zero to one.
» Lift up her head and chest (3-4 months)
» Reach for interesting objects (4-6 months)
» Roll over (4-6 months)
» Sit up (6-8 months)
» Pick something up with two fingers (6-9 months)
» Crawl (6-10 months)
» Pull up on solid objects (9-10 months)
» Stand unsupported / maybe even walk (11-12 months)

two

WHAT'S CHANGING MENTALLY

Want to raise the next Einstein, Newton, or Pythagoras? Check out *Non-Euclidean Geometry for Babies* or *Introductory Calculus for Infants*. Think you may be holding the next Bill Gates, Stephen Wozniak, or Mark Zuckerberg? Make sure to purchase *Web Design for Babies, HTML for Babies, or CSS for Babies*.

It's not hard to find products that can expedite your baby's brainpower and turn them into a certified genius by six months.

But while you are actively training their brain into a million dollar asset, don't forget to be fascinated by some of the basics about how your baby is wired to process information.

HOW YOUR BABY THINKS

At birth, your baby's brain had 100 billion neurons. That's roughly the number of stars in the Milky Way Galaxy.[8] Your baby's brain has all the raw materials it needs to get started, but the next few years will be spent making connections and forming pathways (or synapses) as a result of learning. In the first years of life, your baby's brain will form something like 12,500 synapses per neuron.[9] So even if they aren't composing their first symphony on their third birthday, you can be sure they have still learned a good bit more than the average college freshman.

A newborn's brain accounts for ten percent of their body weight, and it's encased in a head that's roughly 25 percent their total body length.[10]

Another fascinating thing about your baby's brain is that it's mildly aware of everything. Unlike an adult brain, a baby's brain has relatively few inhibitory neurotransmitters. To say it another way, your baby registers just about everything that's happening in the room around them all at once. This lets them take in mass amounts of information quickly, and it makes your baby a creative genius.[11]

HOW YOUR BABY LEARNS

While your baby *is* a genius, your baby doesn't learn like you learn. At the risk of over-simplifying, here are three things to understand about the way your baby learns:

1. BABY'S ACTIONS ARE THEIR THOUGHTS

Actually, a baby's brain learns by exploration.
That means, they learn best by . . .
Seeing
Smelling
Touching
Tasting
Moving
Mimicking
Doing

At this phase, mental development and physical development go hand in hand—or fist in mouth, or toe in ear, or however your baby chooses to discover. One of the best things you can do to help their brain develop is to give your baby opportunities to explore in a safe and controlled environment. "Your overall goal should be not to 'teach' your baby, but to help her discover how to organize experience for herself."[12]

"During the earliest stages, the child perceives things like a solipsist who is unaware of himself as subject and is familiar only with his own actions."

JEAN PIAGET

2. BABIES PREFER THINGS THAT RESPOND TO THEM

Developmental psychologist and philosopher Jean Piaget called babies "egocentric." Maybe you've noticed your little one's preoccupation with his own needs over his sensitivity to your feelings. He really doesn't notice that you've only had four hours of sleep, that you are worried about the grocery bill, and that you haven't showered—if the milk isn't warm enough, he will probably throw it on the floor and start yelling. When it comes to how babies think, you should know this: babies think . . . about themselves.

Your baby divides the world into two categories:
    Things that respond to me
    Things that don't respond to me

(And you guessed it, they learn best from things that respond to them.)

Your baby is a reflexive, responsive learner. They learn and understand the world around them by the responses they get from their actions. This means the best educator for your baby is you. That's just one more reason they "need you now" at this phase more than any other. There just isn't a DVD fancy enough to take your place.

3. BABIES LOVE LANGUAGE

Babies are born with the ability to distinguish all of the world's speech sounds. But as early as four months, your baby will lose that ability in order to focus more specifically on her native language—the language you use to communicate with her.[13]

Just because your conversations seem a little one-sided lately doesn't mean your baby isn't fascinated by your words. In fact, in no other phase of life will your child be as captivated by what you say. Your baby's language development outpaces almost every other area of physical, emotional, mental, and relational development. Simply put, your baby is learning language *FAST*.

YOUR BABY'S LANGUAGE AT A GLANCE

AGE	WHAT THEY UNDERSTAND	HOW THEY COMMUNICATE
0-6 WEEKS	Knows (and prefers) your voice	"CRYING" Has distinctive cries Can make limited vowel sounds
3 MONTHS	Turns toward the sound of your voice	"COOING" Can make consonant sounds like p/b, k/g, m , d , n , w and j
6 MONTHS	Recognizes your tone and can reproduce it Pays attention to music	"BABBLING" Babbles with consonant-vowel-consonant patterns. "ma-ma-ma-ma-ma-ma"
9 MONTHS	Understands simple words like "no" and "bye" through body language Understands words for common objects "cup," "shoe," "milk"	"BABY-SPEAK" Reproduces sounds that you make Babbles with more complex consonant-vowel-consonant or vowel-consonant-vowel patters that resemble native language
12 MONTHS	Understands around 70 words Can follow simple directions— especially when associated with gestures i.e."come with daddy."	"FIRST WORDS" Can pronounce all vowels and about half of the consonant sounds Can say one to four "first words"

SURVIVAL GUIDE

PLAN AN ESCAPE ROUTE

Babies cry most at the gestational age of 46 weeks.[14] So, seize the moment and give those friends and relatives the chance they have been waiting for. Invite them to come watch the baby for an hour. Here's a chart to help you plan your get-away accordingly.

If your baby was...	Expect a lot of crying around...
2 weeks early	8 weeks old
Right on time	6 weeks old
2 weeks late	4 weeks old

PRACTICE YOUR FACES

When babies mimic facial expressions it triggers emotions in them and helps develop their emotional IQ.[15] So keep making those crazy over-the-top happy faces. You are making your baby feel happy—and also probably giving a few other people a good laugh at the same time.

IN CASE YOU HAVEN'T RECEIVED ENOUGH PARENTING ADVICE, HERE ARE A FEW IDEAS TO HELP YOU PARENT THROUGH THE "I NEED YOU NOW" PHASE WITH A UNIQUE KIND OF STYLE.

CHOOSE A NICKNAME

Between five to eight months a baby will recognize their own name and turn to look at you when called.[16] That means you have a short window of time to create a nickname that will really stick.

SIT ON THE RIGHT

Newborns are more likely to turn their head to the right than the left. [17] So if you want to prove you're the "favorite," make sure to position them where your baby's jealous aunt is on the left.

TIME YOUR DIAPER CHANGES

Your baby will require over 2,000 diaper changes this year. On average, women get the job done in 2:05 minutes and men accomplish the task in 1:36 minutes.[18] When you ask for help with diaper duty, know you may have to choose between speed and a thorough wiping.

three

WHAT'S CHANGING CULTURALLY

CULTURE:
the behaviors and beliefs that
characterize a group . . .
or age group.

No one remembers their own birth, but you might imagine it's something like sleeping peacefully in a dark room only to be shaken from your perfect dream when a group of loud giants throw open the shutters, pull back your covers, and turn on the floodlights. No wonder there are a few tears.

BIRTH IS THE FIRST CRISIS OF LIFE

It isn't a bad crisis. In the best cases, a baby enters this world right into the embrace of a loving parent. But even in those indescribably tender moments, something has forever altered the status quo. You know it. And your baby certainly knows it. It's culture shock.

Your baby has suddenly arrived in a world where . . .
no one speaks their language.
they're unsure how to coordinate their movements.
they have limited control over their next meal, their next bath, or their next bowel movement.

You may find that you are suddenly . . .
pumping the brakes at stoplights to "rock" the car.
counting 5 hours of rest as "sleeping through the night."
driving nowhere for an hour and a half because someone fell asleep five minutes before you made it home.

The culture shock is real for you and for your baby. But these cultural changes are an opportunity to discover more about who you are. What's that? You didn't want an "opportunity to discover" this side of yourself? Just remember, on the days that are harder than you anticipated, you also have a love that is much deeper than you might have imagined. And it's that love that will prove strong enough for both you and your baby.

THE BUFFER IN EVERY CRISIS IS LOVE

As you help your baby navigate the changes he will experience these first twelve months, you simply cannot show him too much love. There's no such thing as a spoiled six-month-old. The love you give him lets him know he is safe. You are laying the foundation for how your baby sees the world and his place in it.

YOU HAVE ONE ROLE AT THIS PHASE:

EMBRACE THEIR PHYSICAL NEEDS

When you embrace your baby's physical needs, you . . .
communicate that she is safe,
establish that the world can be trusted,
and demonstrate that she is worth loving.

Your role as a parent will change in the phases to come. But right now, the thing that matters most is how you consistently and lovingly respond to embrace your baby's physical needs.

four

WHAT'S CHANGING RELATIONALLY

One thing you may not know about your baby, from zero to one, is this: they are social. Some may seem more social than others. Some babies seem to "light up" in a room of strangers. Some will reach out to be held by the cashier at the grocery store, or smile at other kids in the waiting room at the pediatrician's office. Others will let you know very clearly when they have had enough oodling and cuddling and passing around to well-intentioned nursery workers or relatives.

But regardless of personality, every baby comes with a social drive.

After four months a baby . . .
» smiles to initiate social contact.
» laughs when you make faces.
» listens to conversations.
» expresses clearly differentiated emotions.

A baby recognizes the voice and smell of her mother from birth. After only two weeks, a baby can visually distinguish his parents from other adults. In the first months, a baby anticipates being lifted and moves her body to participate.

Babies need connection. And right now, in this phase of life, their number one primary relationship is you. In fact, you may never matter more to your child relationally than you do right now.

Don't worry. Your relationship with your son or daughter will become richer and a little more two-sided than it is right now. There just will never be another time in life when they are so utterly fascinated by and dependent on you.

"Life doesn't make any sense without interdependence. We need each other, and the sooner we learn that, the better for us all."

ERIK ERIKSON

You are your child's primary relationship at this phase, so the way you connect with your baby from zero to one lays a foundation for future relational health. Remember, your role is to embrace their physical needs. That role is invaluable because when it comes to your baby's relational changes . . .

YOUR BABY HAS ONE FUNDAMENTAL QUESTION AT THIS PHASE:

AM I SAFE?

Your baby wants to know if she has arrived in a safe place, in a place she can trust. Like everything else she is learning in this phase, the primary way your baby will answer this fundamental question is through experience.[19]

You embrace her physical needs when you . . .
hold her gently,
cuddle her often,
talk to her in a calm or delighted voice,
use her name,
look into her eyes,
or respond to her noises and actions,
When you do any of these things, you are doing something much more significant than you probably realize. You are laying the foundation for your child's future relational health.

YOU HAVE ONE BASIC GOAL AT THIS PHASE:

ESTABLISH TRUST

Around six months, your baby may begin to show signs of stranger wariness. This can make many things in life more complicated, but it might help to know this:

Infants will feel less fearful when . . .
they are in a familiar environment.
they have time to warm up.
the stranger is a female.[20]

This doesn't mean you won't still have some moments of heart-wrenching separation anxiety—both yours and theirs. But the goal is to arrive at a place where separation is possible. The best way to help your child master separation is to give him reliable care while he is with you and allow him the opportunity to experience your consistent return after periods of absence.

Remember, the consistent and loving way you embrace their physical needs now lays the groundwork for future relational stability.

Separation Anxiety begins around six months, peaks at 14 months, and usually resolves by two years.[19]

0 2 4 6 8 10 12 14 16 18 20 22 24

months

ZERO TO ONE

A FEW THINGS ABOUT YOU

In the zero to one phase

$557.60

CHANCES ARE YOU WILL PURCHASE AN AVERAGE OF 2,788 DIAPERS FOR A TOTAL COST OF $557.60[22]

ON AVERAGE, YOU WILL SLEEP 350-400 FEWER HOURS THIS YEAR THAN YOU HAVE IN PREVIOUS YEARS.[23]

THE MORE TIME YOU SPEND WITH YOUR BABY, THE HIGHER YOUR OPINION WILL BE ABOUT YOUR BABY'S ABILITIES.[24]

→ # DID YOU KNOW?

A FEW THINGS ABOUT **THEM**

In the zero to one phase

BABIES PAY ATTENTION TO OBJECTS LONGER IF THEY KNOW THE WORD FOR THE OBJECT.[25]

DURING THE FIRST THREE YEARS OF LIFE, A BABY'S BRAIN GROWS AND DEVELOPS MORE THAN AT ANY OTHER CONCENTRATED TIME IN LIFE.

BY HIS FIRST BIRTHDAY, YOUR BABY IS LIKELY TO UNDERSTAND ABOUT 70 WORDS.[26]

YOUR BABY HAS 100 MORE BONES IN HER BODY THAN YOU DO. SOME BONES ACTUALLY FUSE TOGETHER AS YOUR BABY GROWS, REDUCING THE NUMBER FROM 300 TO 206.[27]

UP UNTIL SEVEN MONTHS OLD, A BABY CAN BREATHE AND SWALLOW AT THE SAME TIME. (YOU JUST TRIED IT, DIDN'T YOU?) [28]

five

WHAT'S CHANGING EMOTIONALLY

Your baby is emotional.

For some of you, your baby may seem more emotional than others. But the fact is all babies are emotional because all people are emotional. And that's actually a good thing. Emotions are both universal and helpful.

Think about it.
When you see a bee, you feel fear, and you move away. *When you hear thunder*, you feel curious. You look up, notice the rain clouds, and go inside. *When you see blue lights in your rearview mirror*, you panic, hit the brakes, and put your hands at the perfect ten-and-two position on the steering wheel.

Emotions help organize our behavior. They are a mixture of physical and social responses that help us adjust to our environment.[29]

But just because your baby is emotional doesn't mean your baby experiences the myriad of complex emotions you do. (You can look forward to some of those emotions in another phase.)

YOU BABY IS DISCOVERING NEW EMOTIONS

From birth, infants experience just two basic emotions: pleasure and distress. But by nine months, a baby will experience all of the basic emotions: anger, disgust, fear, happiness, sadness, and surprise.[30]

In some ways your baby's basic emotional development, like physical development, is easier to understand because you can see it. According to

Paul Ekman, a pioneer in the psychology of emotions, these basic emotions all have universal facial expressions that make them easily identifiable.

LOOK FOR THE SIGNS:

Day one – expressing distress . . . *you will recognize it.*

6 weeks – the first social smile

2 months – mirroring expressions of anger or sadness

4 months – expressing disgust . . . probably as you introduce your baby to a new food

6 months – turning away from strangers to show fear

7 months – smiling with the hope of encouraging interaction

7 months – expressing surprise with sudden movements or loud noises

YOUR BABY IS EXPERIENCING YOUR EMOTIONS

As babies move from zero to one, they experience an increasingly wider range of emotions. Infants also match their emotions to the emotions they observe in other people.[31] That means your baby watches you for social cues. By four months, infants can distinguish happy faces from sad faces.[32] And when your baby mimics your facial expressions, it triggers emotions in them.[33] Studies show, for example, that babies are more likely to play with a new toy if their parent smiles when the toy is introduced. In the same way, if leaving your child at the church nursery or with a day-care worker or with your own mother causes you distress, it's likely to cause them distress. Babies learn how to respond to other people, objects, and situations by observing how you respond.[34]

For some of you, knowing that your baby is mirroring your emotions can be stressful—which probably means you're stressing your baby out just by reading this section. Relax. Nobody is 100% emotionally stable 100% of the time—and that's without the sleep deprivation you feel. You are human. And your baby is also resilient. But if you want to help your child develop emotional stability, both in this phase and the phases to come, remember to take care of yourself. You may just be a little more capable with an extra hour of rest and a shower.

six

WHAT'S CHANGING MORALLY

It may seem strange to talk about the morality of your baby. Chances are they haven't come to you with suggestions for starting a non-profit or asked that you donate their extra Cheerios.

YOUR BABY EXPERIENCES MORAL EMOTIONS NATURALLY

You might be surprised at the many ways your baby is forming impressions about the world around her—even from zero to one. According to developmental molecular biologist John Medina, your baby was actually born "pre-loaded" with "limited moral sensibilities."[35] It's as if somehow in God's plan, the stamp of His image still affects us. Even though babies regularly demonstrate their inherent self-centered nature, they also come with a remarkable ability to recognize good and prefer it over evil. Our from-birth morality is like a compass leading us in the direction of the One who made us.

Studies of babies actually show some remarkable things about the phenomenon of baby morality. Using puppets, researchers observe:

by 5 months babies show a preference for good over bad.
by 8 months babies demonstrate signs for understanding justice.[36]

Studies like these indicate that babies experience "moral" emotions. You might notice this in a nursery with multiple babies. When one baby starts to cry, there is often a domino effect. The emotion is contagious.

YOUR BABY'S MORAL REASONING IS LIMITED MENTALLY

It's probably important to note that moral *emotions* are different from moral *reasoning*. Just because your baby may smile at the good and frown at the bad, or cry when they hear the distress of another baby, doesn't mean he is ready to enter into a moral debate.

A child can't reason morally beyond their ability to reason intellectually.

Remember: Babies are egocentric.
They aren't aware of multiple perspectives.

That means true empathetic, put-myself-in-your-shoes reasoning is off the table for now. It's normal for your baby to think about himself. It's all in the way his brain is wired at this phase. Just because he smiles at himself in the mirror doesn't mean you are raising a narcissist.

YOUR BABY FORMS MORAL IMPRESSIONS RELATIONALLY

Throughout adolescence and into adulthood, we learn right from wrong, acceptable from unacceptable, through our relationships with others. In the same way, a child will begin to develop moral impressions by observing you.

Your baby watches your social cues to discover what makes you feel happy, sad, angry, or disappointed. Even though this isn't forming a logical moral reasoning in them, they are developing first impressions of what is good.

Even beyond first impressions, some research suggests you can provide your baby with opportunities to develop precursory skills that will shape their future moral abilities. Specifically, you can help your baby with . . .

      focus   self-control   self-soothing.[37]

It's okay if your baby doesn't win a Nobel Peace Prize this year. As you embrace their physical needs to help them feel safe, they will understand more about the nature of love.

ZERO TO ONE

YOUR ROLE:

THEIR QUESTION:

YOUR GOAL:

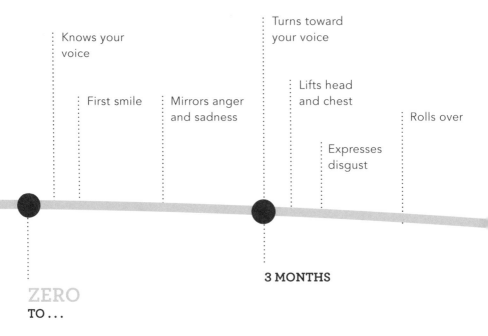

Knows your voice

First smile

Mirrors anger and sadness

Turns toward your voice

Lifts head and chest

Expresses disgust

Rolls over

3 MONTHS

ZERO
TO ...

AT A GLANCE

EMBRACE THEIR PHYSICAL NEEDS

"AM I SAFE?"

ESTABLISH TRUST

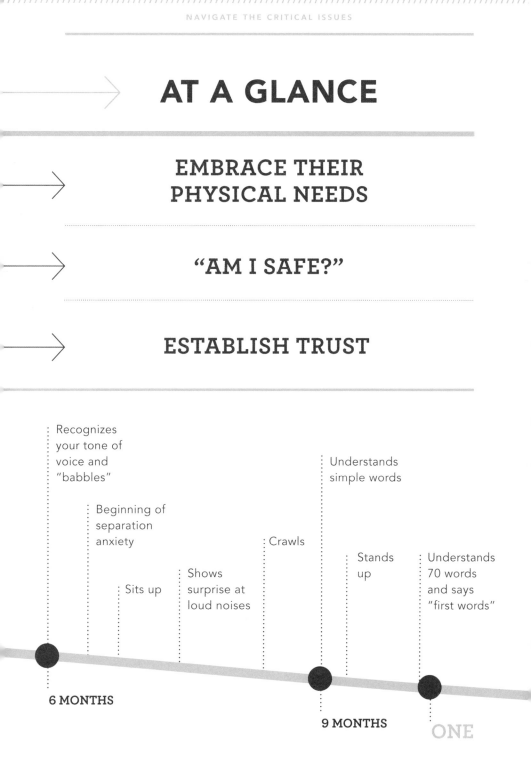

Recognizes your tone of voice and "babbles"

Beginning of separation anxiety

Sits up

Shows surprise at loud noises

Crawls

Understands simple words

Stands up

Understands 70 words and says "first words"

6 MONTHS

9 MONTHS

ONE

LEVE

THE **SIX THINGS**

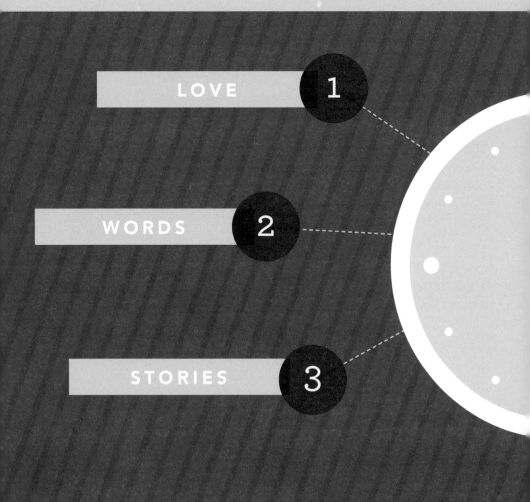

LOVE — 1

WORDS — 2

STORIES — 3

RAGE

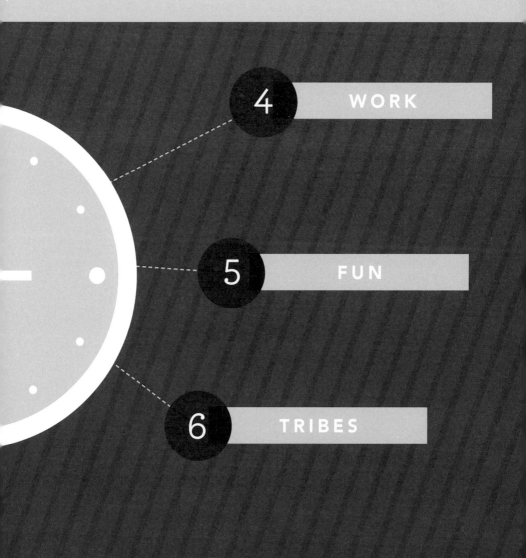

4   WORK

5   FUN

6   TRIBES

Now that you know a little more about your growing baby you might be wondering, what does it all mean? Before picking up this book you probably thought your baby's needs were obvious:
food,
sleep,
comfort,
and a clean diaper.

You're right. That's why your role in this phase is to embrace their physical needs. You are in the business of establishing trust so your baby will know she is safe. But how you practically carry this out comes down to six things your baby needs that you might not have considered before. Actually, we think these are the six things every kid needs at every phase:

LOVE, WORDS, STORIES, WORK, FUN, TRIBES

WEEKS

Before you hit the panic button, these six things are actually pretty simple (a lot simpler than trying to comfort a colicky baby). And when you know how to give your child these same six things through every phase, they will help you build history together. They will help you pass on an everyday faith. They will lay the groundwork for giving your child . . .

WORTH, DIRECTION, PERSPECTIVE, PURPOSE, CONNECTION, BELONGING

This section will give you practical suggestions and interactive opportunities to consider how you can use the six things to influence your baby from zero to one.

SO DON'T MISS THE DISTINCTIVE OPPORTUNITIES OF ...

ZERO TO ONE

TIME MATTERS

When we wrote the book *Playing for Keeps*, we challenged parents with a meaningful task: We gave parents a jar filled with 936 marbles and asked them to reduce the number of marbles in the jar to the actual number of weeks their child had left at home before graduation. Their next long-term assignment was to remove one marble each week.

For those parents, the jar became a constant visual reminder of something that's absolutely essential if you want to influence a kid or teenager: TIME.

There's nothing special about a jar of marbles.
But something happens when you quantify the amount of time you have left with your kid.

When you see how much time you have left, you tend to do more with the time you have now.

936 marbles may seem like a lot.
Right now it may seem like your baby will never sleep through the night. Potty training feels like a million years away. And the idea of high school graduation simply hadn't crossed your mind . . . yet.

But it will go by fast.

We're not trying to depress you. Or say something that's a little cliché in the Zero to One Phase. (How many times have you had someone tell you to treasure this phase because it won't last forever?)

But it's true.
You will only know your baby once as a newborn.
Next year he or she will be walking and talking and drawing on the wall with a Sharpie.

Putting a visual number to the time you have left isn't a new idea.
One shrewd leader said it this way:

"Teach us to number our days, that we may gain a heart of wisdom"

PSALM 90:12

So, how does counting your days give you a heart of wisdom?
We're not sure.
But we can guess.

Think about what happens with the countdown clock in a basketball game.
As the clock gets closer to zero, the intensity increases.
The players become more focused.

In the same way, visualizing the time you have with your kid may help you . . .
pace yourself,
narrow your focus,
guard your margin,
value quality interaction,
and become more intentional about what you do.

When you see how much time you have left,
you tend to value what happens over time.

The jar of marbles is also a reminder of the potential you have when you consider how you are investing in your child over multiple weeks.

What you do this week matters, but you can't get it all done this week. That's why it takes a collection of weeks to parent a child.

When you give your child love, words, stories, work, fun, and tribes—
over time . . .
they gain collective momentum.
they make history.
they build a legacy.

So count down the number of weeks you have with your baby before their graduation day.

Hint: If you want to use a cheat, download the free "legacy countdown" app and enter your child's birthday and you will see a more accurate number of weeks specific for your baby.

Once you know the number, select a container and fill it with the appropriate number of marbles, coins, paper clips, M&M's®, Jelly Belly's®, gum balls, etc. (Warning: Edible items may disappear faster than a week at a time).

Then, create a family ritual of removing one item from the container each week as a simple reminder that . . .
time is moving,
every week counts,
and the collection of weeks will influence your child more than you can presently understand.

6 THINGS KIDS NEED OVER TIME

1 LOVE/TIME =
WORTH

2 STORIES/TIME =
PERSEVERANCE

3 FUN/TIME =
CONNECTION

4 WORDS/TIME =
DIRECTION

5 WORK/TIME =
SIGNIFICANCE

6 TRIBES/TIME =
BELONGING

one

LOVE/TIME
= WORTH

BE PHYSICALLY AND CONSISTENTLY PRESENT

"Love can change a person the way a parent can change

a baby—awkwardly, and often with a great deal of mess."

LEMONY SNICKET, *HORSERADISH*

SHOW UP

It's hard *not to* show up—especially when your baby is utterly dependent on you just to eat, sleep, and stay reasonably clean. Besides, if you don't show up fast enough, your baby's built-in alarm system may activate and alert the entire neighborhood.

Don't underestimate the significance of your physical presence. It's more than just de-activating their crying. Even though your three-month-old may not say "thank you" or make you a special card to celebrate your efforts, the attention you give now is making physiological and psychological differences that will impact their future and their faith.

Brain research shows the more consistently a baby receives loving support—especially during times of stress—the larger and more developed the social portion of a baby's brain becomes.[38] *Psychological studies* show that the more consistently a parent shows up and responds to their baby, the more trusting the child will be in later phases. *Spiritual development* suggests that establishing trust in early years lays a foundation for later faith.

Simply put: You cannot give your baby too much love.
So keep showing up. You are giving your baby the love they need every time you . . .
» smile and make eye contact.
» touch your nose to their nose.
» make silly faces.
» wiggle their toes.
» imitate their babbles.
» sing a lullaby.
» give them a shoulder to sleep on.
» pick them up when they cry.
» show up to let them know you care.

KNOW THEM
Your baby isn't like every baby.
The way you show up and love your baby won't be exactly like anyone else.

Some babies like to be held.
Some babies like to be set down.

Some babies like to be bundled up.
Some babies like to have more freedom.

Some babies are born on a schedule.
Some babies defy a schedule at every turn.

When it comes to loving your baby, it's more about knowing what works for the two of you than it is about following any prescribed formula. If this isn't your first baby, you may have already discovered the difference that can exist between two babies—even in the same family!

As you get to know what makes your baby unique, write down a few of the preferences you notice.

LIKES:

....

....

....

....

....

DISLIKES:

....

....

....

....

....

FUNNY QUIRKS:

....

....

....

....

....

SET BOUNDARIES

You can't "spoil" your baby with too much attention at this phase.
It's just not possible . . . *yet*. That means there's very little sense in trying
various forms of discipline strategies before your baby's first birthday.[39]
Shortly after that first cake, you will be running to the experts for some
boundary-setting advice—fast.

For now, some of the best boundaries you can set are for yourself.
It's easy to neglect self-care from zero to one, but the way you take care of
yourself matters for you, and it matters for your child.

During this phase make sure to . . .
find a consistent community.
schedule time away.
ask for help.

No matter what your situation, whether you have limited finances, you're
a single parent, or you live far away from any extended family, self-care
is essential. You may have to get creative in the ways you create margin
for yourself, but you need it. Reach out to a grandparent. Connect with
a local church. Find a trusted neighbor. Babies need loving care, and in
order to provide that kind of care for your baby, you need to care for
yourself as well.

two

WORDS/TIME
= DIRECTION

SPEAK THE WORDS THEY NEED TO HEAR

"The only thing we know of, that makes babies smarter, is talking to them."

LISE ELLIOT

IMPROVE YOUR PRACTICAL VOCABULARY

Your baby *loves* the sound of *your* voice. In fact, no one has ever wanted to listen to you more than your baby. If you've been waiting your whole life for someone to hang on your every word, now's your chance, your golden moment. So seize it. It won't last forever.

Talk to your baby. In phases to come, your child will use words to think. Which means, the more words they know, the more they can understand and imagine. One of the most practical gifts you are giving your child this year is the gift of your words.

As you speak to your baby keep it: Simple, Clear, and Repetitive.
If you want even more ideas on how to accelerate your baby's language, consider the following:

0 - 3 Months	Babble with your baby by making eye contact and repeating syllables.
3 - 6 Months	Point at objects and name them. Use one word. Repeat it. Start with nouns and verbs. Use gestures (or sign language) to accompany common words.[40]
6 - 9 Months	Begin naming simple prepositions (on, off, in, out), adjectives (big, yellow, bumpy), adverbs (quietly, loudly, fast, slow), and pronouns (me, you, him, her). If you want to know what these words are, just check out *Go, Dog, Go* at the library and let that be your manual.
9 - 12 Months	Tell your baby what you are doing. Talk to your baby about what they are doing.

Continue using lots of repetition. Remember, children learn at different paces. Don't get discouraged. There is usually a five-month gap between when your baby learns the meaning of a word and when he will first speak the word.[41] So even if you don't have a big talker, your baby is learning your language.

IMPROVE YOUR RELATIONAL VOCABULARY

Words can draw people together or push them apart. They can send messages of approval or distain. They can motivate or deter. Improving your relational vocabulary in the first year of life is pretty simple. Your baby doesn't need a motivational speech or a lengthy explanation of his strengths.

Your baby needs positive language, in an elevated pitch, with a happy expression. The tone of your voice matters even more than the specific words you say during this phase—babies are highly sensitive to your emotions. You can delight your baby with your words when you speak to him with an elevated pitch, a smile, and eye contact.

IMPROVE YOUR SPIRITUAL VOCABULARY

In the same way your child will use words to think, your child will use words to think about God and about faith. So, use basic faith vocabulary in your home.

Talk about God.
"Look at the tree that God made," or
"Who made your belly button? God made your belly button."

Talk about Church.
"That is a church."
"Did you go to church?"

Using words like God, Church, Jesus, Pray, and Bible with your baby from zero to one will give them the foundation for spiritual conversations in the phases to come.

Sing Songs.
Another way to begin your baby's spiritual vocabulary is through song. Simple melodies can put spiritual vocabulary in a calm and loving context.

You don't have to be a good singer. You don't even have to be able to hold a tune for your baby to be mesmerized by the sound of your singing voice. (That won't be true a few years from now).

Singing can be fun when you greet your baby in the morning, during bath time, or as a lullaby just before bed. So, sing.

»   Sing songs you remember from your childhood.
»   Buy an album or look up songs online.
»   Make up a song as you go.

Or simply use one of these:
"Jesus Loves Me"
"Taps (Day is Done)"
"Jesus Loves the Little Children"
"Amazing Grace"

What are some songs you could sing now that will help your baby hear basic spiritual truths?

....
....
....
....
....
....
....
....
....
....
....
....
....
....
....
....
....

three

STORIES/TIME
= PERSPECTIVE

SELECT STORIES TO INSPIRE THEM

"Someday you will be old enough to start reading fairy tales again."

C.S. LEWIS

HIGHLIGHT CULTURAL STORIES

Make a regular practice of reading to your baby—even if it's *Sports Illustrated*, *Fast Company*, or your Facebook newsfeed. Sound crazy? Not really. Reading out loud to your child is one of the best practices you can establish—even in the first twelve months—that will last for years to come. So, set aside a time every day to hold them and read for just a few minutes.

BOOKS

Of course, there are some things that are better to read than others. Typically, things with **rhyming, repetition, colors, textures,** or **pictures** will go over well. Below are some of our suggestions:

"PAT THE BUNNY"
Dorothy Kunhardt

"THAT'S NOT MY DINOSAUR"
Fiona Watt

"THE GOING TO BED BOOK"
Sandra Boynton

"BLACK ON WHITE"
Tana Hoban

"LLAMA LLAMA NIGHTY-NIGHT"
Anna Dewdney

"BABY CAKES"
Karma Wilson

"BROWN BEAR, BROWN BEAR, WHAT DO YOU SEE?"
Bill Martin, Jr.

"WHERE IS BABY'S BELLY BUTTON"
Karen Katz

"CHICKA CHICKA BOOM BOOM"
Bill Martin, Jr.

"FIRST WORDS"
Roger Priddy

"MOO, BA, LA, LA, LA"
Sandra Boynton

"THE VERY HUNGRY CATERPILLAR"
Eric Carle

CAPTURE FAMILY STORIES

It's hard to believe it, but you won't remember this phase in a year or two. You can't stop your baby from growing up, but you can record a few things about your baby now so you can remember them later. You don't have to do it all. But try to choose one or two things that you can do this year.

Take monthly (or quarterly) photos.
Fill in a few pages of a baby book.
Make handprints or footprints.
Start a journal written to your child.
Make a scrapbook.
Fill a shoebox with keepsakes.

Even if you aren't a baby book making, scrapbooking, journaling type, you can record something about this phase. There's no shortage of ways to document the first years of a baby's life. And if you want a little assistance here are a few tools to help you.

Go online and check out websites like: *Momentific, Shutterfly, or Peekaboo.* Download Apps like: *Second Everyday, ShutterCal, Moment Garden, Tiny Beans, Bambio, or My iStory.*

How have you recorded or documented other memorable events in your past? What are some things you want to record and remember about these first twelve months, and how can you do that?

....

....

....

....

....

....

SHARE FAITH STORIES

This year, you will read stories about bears and llamas and caterpillars. You will also read books that name emotions, body parts, and familiar household objects. You will introduce your baby to non-fiction and fiction without ever second-guessing whether the hungry caterpillar will forever confuse them about the dietary habits of insects.

That's because in later phases your child will begin to distinguish imagination from reality. But for now, don't overthink it. It's okay to read Cinderella and Noah's Ark.

Read some Bible stories.

They won't remember the name of the characters. They don't understand the theological significance. For now, just enjoy sharing faith stories with your child that have a special meaning for you, knowing they will someday come to love these stories the way you do.

As you select Bible stories to read with your baby, look for the same qualities they enjoy in other stories:

rhyming, repetition, colors, textures, and pictures.

four

WORK/TIME = PURPOSE

GIVE THEM PRACTICAL RESPONSIBILITIES

"The greatest gifts you can give your children are the roots of responsibility and the wings of independence."

DENIS WAITLEY

GIVE THEM SOMETHING TO DO

Most of this year, you will find yourself wondering, "When can they _____ on their own?" Your biggest transition is to adjust to a life where someone needs you so *often*, so *immediately*, so *desperately*.

But just remember, there are some things they can do on their own. And it's actually important to let them do it. The struggle to hold their head up now will show them there is a reward for work. And it will show you that even though your child will need you for the rest of their life, they won't need you to rescue them from the struggles that help them value hard work and determination.

A few things your baby will do all by himself this year:

» Hold their head up
» Get back to sleep (self soothing)
» Roll over
» Sit up
» Crawl
» Stand up
» Pick things up (fine motor skills)
» First steps (well...they might not)

Add to this list. What can your baby do? When did you discover they could do it?

....

....

....

....

....

....

....

....

....

....

....

IN THE PHASES TO COME YOU WILL
GIVE THEM SOMETHING TO OWN

It's too soon to give your two-month-old their own . . .

Allowance
Checking account
Car

In this phase you can set some financial goals. What can you do now to get yourself in a better place financially? How can you prepare for the expenses you know are coming in the phases ahead? What are your realistic goals or expectations for funding major expenses like education, a car, a wedding, etc...?

Someday, when you've eaten, showered, slept, AND no one is crying, write down three financial goals that will help you give your baby a better future.

1.

....

....

2.

....

....

3.

....

....

IN THE PHASES TO COME YOU WILL
GIVE THEM SOMEWHERE TO SERVE

In the same way that it's too soon to let your baby practice good financial habits, it's too soon to give them opportunities to serve. You probably aren't going to sign your newborn up for service hours at a local shelter.

In this phase you can let someone serve you. It takes humility sometimes. The way you let others serve you now can influence how you and your child serve others later. (WARNING: This might mean you have to open the door to someone on a day when your house is a disaster and you haven't showered or eaten all day, and you're likely to breakdown in tears if they give you a casserole . . . not that we've ever done that in real life. That would be embarrassing.)

five

FUN/TIME
= CONNECTION

PLAY AND LAUGH TOGETHER MORE OFTEN

"Babies should be classified as an antidepressant. It's pretty hard to be in a bad mood around a 5-month-old baby."

JIM GAFFIGAN

LEARN WHAT THEY LIKE

In the first twelve months, most of your baby's playtime will last under ten minutes, and you will be close by if not directly involved. That doesn't mean you shouldn't encourage some individual playtime for your baby when you can. You should. Playing alone actually encourages independence, self-confidence, creativity, and language skills.[42] When you set your baby down to play, offer objects to encourage fun.

LOOSEN UP

In addition to independent play, your baby craves interactive play—specifically with you. So play together! It can be as simple as getting on the floor and playing with some of the toys listed on the next page. Or play can happen with few or no toys involved.

ZERO
— TO —
ONE

TOYS

Most of the toys that will engage your baby in independent play during the first year will have **lights, sounds,** or **textures.**

MOBILES AND
BOUNCY SEATS
(1-6 months)

RATTLES AND
PLASTIC KEY RINGS
(3-12 months)

STACKING RINGS
(12 months)

TAG BLANKETS
(1-12 months)

SOMETHING THAT
PLAYS MUSIC
(3-12 months)

SHAPE SORTERS
(12 months)

PLAY MATS WITH
INTERESTING
TEXTURES
(1-12 months)

AN EXERSAUCER
(7-12 months)

BIG BLOCKS
(12 months)

PLUSH TOYS AND
TEDDY BEARS
(3-12 months)

"MUSICAL" POTS
AND PANS
(7-12 months)

ANYTHING WITH
A MIRROR
(4 months-forever)

You will know you are getting an A+ in play if both you and your baby are laughing. So figure out what it is that makes you laugh, and set aside some time to do more of that every week. Here are some ideas to help get you started:

» Peek-a-boo
» Silly noises
» Crazy faces
» Drop it/Pick it up
» Finger puppets
» Bubbles
» Passing objects back and forth
» Naming opposites

What are some other games you have discovered that make you and your baby laugh?

....

....

....

....

....

....

....

....

LOSE THE AGENDA

Play can bolster brain development. The right toys can raise IQ and expedite motor skills. Interactive games can foster social awareness. But just be careful not to turn "results" into the reason for your child's play.

Sometimes babies (and people) need to have fun—just because it's fun.

Even if the fun seems silly.
Even if the fun lacks purpose.
Even if the fun doesn't lead to learning.
It's still worth it to JUST HAVE FUN.

When you have fun together with your baby, you show your baby that you are interested in them. You demonstrate that you like them. You let them know they are worth playing with. And as you create these moments of play, you may be giving your child something that's even more significant than a genius IQ or advanced motor development. You are giving them connection. So, each week remember to set aside some time for fun.

six

TRIBES/TIME
= BELONGING

HELP THEM EXPERIENCE COMMUNITY

"Family faces are magic mirrors. Looking at people who belong to us, we see the past, present, and future."

GAIL LUMET BUCKLEY

CREATE APPEALING SPACES

Every tribe has a place. The environment where your family eats and sleeps and plays together has incredible potential to connect you relationally, to communicate values, and to establish rhythms to your day.

Whether your baby's nursery looks like a replica of something you saw on Pinterest, an eclectic assembly of second-hand furnishings, or your own thematic creation complete with a hand-drawn mural, one thing is probably true: You created an appealing space for your baby before she ever arrived.

Now that your baby is here, it's important to think about more than just an appealing nursery.

Create designated spaces in your home where your child can Play, Eat, Wind Down, and Sleep. Babies associate environments with a particular routine, behavior, or expectation. So, it's important to not only create distinct environments, but to establish predictable behavioral patterns within those spaces. How would you complete the following statements?

Every time my baby is ...., we play together.

When my baby is ...., she has independent playtime.

Every time my baby is ...., he eats something.

Every time my baby is ...., she is expected to sleep (and not play).

Of course you will have exceptions to the rule. Some days your baby may nap in the car seat. Some days you may feed your baby while you are in the living room watching the Big Game. Some days you may accidently both fall asleep at the kitchen table—it could happen.

Ideally, you will have some spaces in your home that are distinctly designed to meet at least three needs for your baby: Eating, Playing, and Sleeping. Create spaces to accommodate those activities, and try to keep the exceptions the exception.

ESTABLISH SHARED TRADITIONS

Whether you are a single parent, an adoptive-parent, a multi-generational family, a blended family, or a mixture of all the above, your family will be the most significant tribe your child will ever belong to. Nothing has more influence on a child than family.

And one of the things that makes your family *your* family are the traditions that you share.

TRADITION:
a repeated
pattern of behavior

Some family traditions happen annually (like holidays and birthdays).
We will talk more about those in the next section.

Some traditions happen within the rhythm of your week.
They can be as simple as the way you . . .
pray with your baby at bedtime.
greet your baby with the same phrase each morning.
sing a familiar song as you brush their teeth (or gums really).
say a familiar rhyme as you change their diaper or give them a bath.

The traditions that you establish in the first twelve months of your baby's
life may not remain the same over the next eighteen years. In fact,
they probably shouldn't. But it's still important to have a few repeated
behaviors that give your child a sense of security, draw you closer
together as a family, and communicate the values of your tribe.

How would you complete the following statement?

In our family, we . . .

....

....

....

....

....

RECRUIT POSITIVE INFLUENCES

Child development theorists, politicians (left or right), psychologists, spiritual formation experts, and bloggers likely don't agree about much, but there is one thing they all seem to be on board with: A child has a better future when there are three to five adults who consistently show up and care for them.[43]

It may seem like with all the emphasis on *your* role during the "I need *you* now" phase, it's a little too soon to begin recruiting other adult influences. But some research suggests that even in the first twelve months of life, spending time with non-parental caregivers helps infants learn to read different facial expressions and expand their ability to take the perspectives of others.[44] So, maybe it's never too early to begin to think about the community you want for your baby as they grow.

In the Zero to One Phase, *you* are in control of recruiting other adult influences. So be proactive.

Let your baby . . .
»   spend time with extended family.
»   get to know a neighbor or close friend.
»   have a consistent hour each week in the church nursery.

Name three to five adults who have influence with you and your baby in this phase.

....

....

....

....

....

CELE

THE BIG MOMENTS

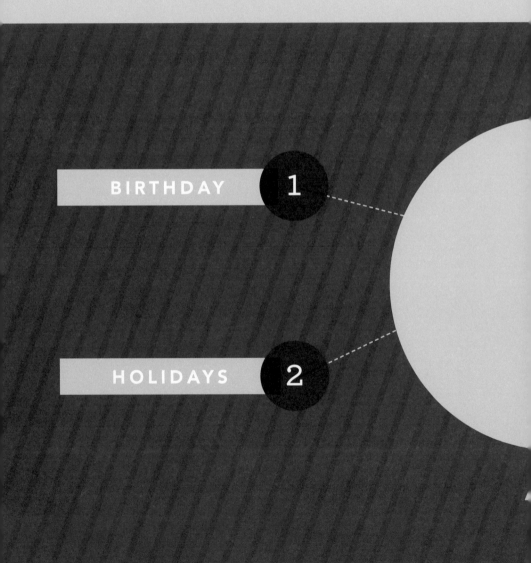

BIRTHDAY 1

HOLIDAYS 2

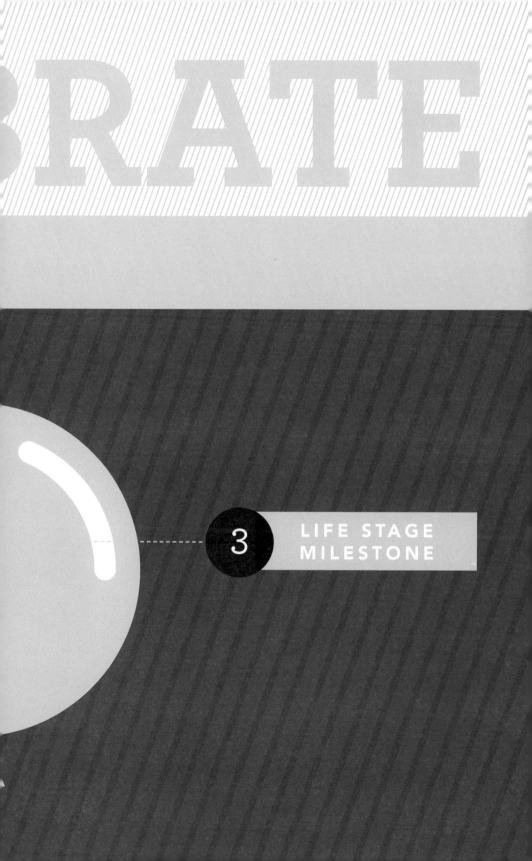

RATE

3

LIFE STAGE
MILESTONE

What you do every week matters.
And what you do every week matters more when it happens *over time*.

But there are some moments that only come around seasonally, annually, or once in a lifetime. And the way you celebrate those moments have a different kind of impact.

Over the next eighteen years with your child, some moments will . . .

create a shared experience.
mark a significant milestone.
begin an annual tradition.

When we asked parents to create a digital countdown clock, we gave them a few marbles that were unlike the rest. Every jar of marbles came with eighteen birthday marbles and one unique marble for each of six milestone events: dedication, first day of school, salvation, transition, driver's license, and graduation.

The reason was simple.
All weeks aren't created equal.

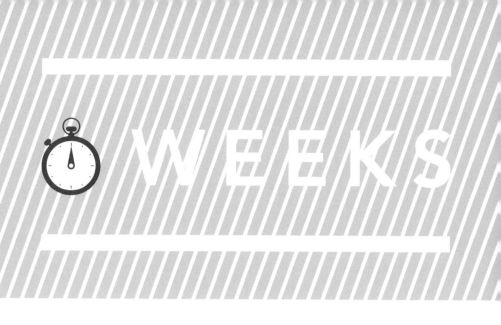

WEEKS

You will only have one first birthday party, one first Christmas, one baby dedication.

In this section, we will give you a few practical ideas to get you thinking about how you might celebrate these big moments in unique and memorable ways.

SO DON'T MISS
THE DISTINCTIVE
OPPORTUNITIES OF ...

ZERO
TO
ONE

one

BIRTHDAY

You have eighteen of these special days with your child while they're with you. So, it's probably a good idea to start a few birthday traditions. Your traditions could be passed down from your own history, or you can steal from others on Facebook, Pinterest, or parenting blogs. Here are a few traditions we've seen that you could begin, even on their very special first birthday.

Birthday Eve Story Time: On the night before a birthday, share the story of your child's arrival. How did you find out your baby was on the way? What are your memories of this day, one year ago? Light a candle and blow it out to say good-bye to the past year.

An Annual Birthday Playlist: Talk about the music you have enjoyed playing for your child this year. What songs did they respond to?

Create a playlist of favorite music from their first year.

....

....

....

....

Record a Birthday Toast: At dinner or during cake, have each family member or guest share something that makes the birthday girl/boy special. Record a video of the toasts, or have guest write their toasts in letters for your child to read later.

Write your toast here.

....

....

....

....

....

Your child will only turn one once. That can seem like a lot of pressure. You have one day to . . .
take the perfect "first birthday" picture.
have just the right "first birthday" cake.
create the best "first birthday" keepsake.

But relax. Let's admit it. **Your baby's first birthday is more about you than them.** Even though it's a party to celebrate your child's first year of life, they actually won't remember the decorations or count their gifts. They won't get upset if you don't invite their "best friend." They will simply be happy to have a day with you and maybe get to taste a little cake.

So . . .
If you like to throw a big party and host many guests, go for it!
If you prefer a smaller setting with just family, enjoy keeping it simple.
If you love to decorate for special events, let your creativity go wild.
If you get stressed out by spending "un-necessarily," don't.
Do what fits your style.

two

HOLIDAYS

From zero to one, the calendar holidays may look a lot more like the average weekday than ever before. Just like every other day, you will find yourself diapering, feeding, swaddling, and bathing your adorable little bundle. But just because the "everyday" is still a part of the holiday doesn't mean you won't do a few things to make those moments special.

EASTER

There's a good chance your baby won't comprehend the meaning of this significant day, but you can still celebrate in a special way. Go to church. Read a board book about the meaning of Easter. Sing "Jesus Loves Me." Use this as a day to talk about just how much God loves us.

HALLOWEEN

This may be the only year when you are 100% in control of your baby's costume. Turn them into a cabbage patch kid. Wrap them up like a pumpkin. Put them inside an un-lit jack 'o lantern. There really is no limit to the fun photo-ops this holiday provides.

THANKSGIVING

Your baby may, or may not, be able to share the savory tastes of this holiday this year, but you can surround yourself with family and friends . . . and take an extra nap while grandma is around to change the diapers.

CHRISTMAS

This may be one of the best holidays to create some family traditions. Whether your traditions remain constant or change with the phases, go ahead and try a few this year and make your baby's first Christmas one to remember.

Four Gift Ideas: If you are wary of too many gifts for one little baby, or you don't want your home filled with loud noise makers and bright plastic obstacles to trip over, ask doting friends and relatives to choose gifts that fit in one of four categories: something they want, something they need, something they wear, something they read.

One Gift Tradition: Start a tradition of new Christmas pajamas on Christmas Eve, a special Christmas ornament to put on the tree, or a Christmas book to read before bed.

Nativity Story-Time: If you have a nativity in your home, show your baby the different pieces as you set up the scene. Talk about the characters and tell the story as you put the pieces in place.

A Christmas Keepsake: Commemorate "baby's first Christmas" by making (or purchasing) something special this year that you will bring out every Christmas. Make a handprint. Get a special ornament. Take a picture. Create a memory book. Do whatever fits your style.

OTHER PARTY DAYS

Just because the rest of the world isn't making a BIG deal out of a holiday doesn't mean you can't start some celebration traditions of your own. If you're having a case of the baby-blues, pick a day. Make your own celebration! Here are a few days that might be perfect for a zero to one party.

Bubble Bath Day:	Jan 8
National Siblings Day:	April 10
National Splurge Day:	June 18
Teddy Bear Picnic Day:	July 10
Cousins Day:	July 24

three

LIFE STAGE MILESTONE

LIFE STAGE MILESTONE:
an event that marks and celebrates a
significant moment or change in a person's
development.

BEGINNING: BABY DEDICATION

The first phases of a kid's life are unique and exciting. It's the beginning. That's why one of the six Life Stage milestones you might want to celebrate is a Baby Dedication. Depending on your denomination or faith history, you may use another name (like christening or even baptism), and the event may confer additional meaning to the event.

But in the simplest definition, we simply mean this:

Baby Dedication is a moment in time when you publicly commit to parenting with the future faith of your child in mind.

When you celebrate a Baby Dedication, you create a moment outside the day-to-day chaos of sleep schedules and feeding battles to imagine the life you want for your baby in the years to come. You move outside the immediate issues at hand and prioritize the things that matter most.

You imagine the end.

Imagining the end means looking into the future to the day when this tiny bundle you now cuddle on your chest has a driver's license and a diploma in hand. Consider the things you want to be true in their life when you help them move into a dorm room or first apartment.
Who do you want them to be?
What do you hope your relationship will look like?
How do you want them to remember their growing up years?

Imagining the end may be one of the most important things you can do as a parent in the first years of your child's life. It will be the thing in the years to come that will help you stay focused, prioritize, and maintain perspective.

Even if it doesn't happen in the first twelve months, consider selecting a date on your calendar to have a Baby Dedication event sometime in the first years of your baby's life. Here are just a few ideas that could help you celebrate this once in a lifetime moment.

INVITE SIGNIFICANT PEOPLE

Use this time to celebrate the ways other people have invested in your own life. Let them know you will need them to help you parent this child. Invite them into the process because there will come a day in the not so distant future when you will no longer be enough, and the other adults in your child's life will take on a more significant role.

Make a list of people who invested in your life who you want to invite to your Baby Dedication.

....

....

....

CLARIFY WHAT MATTERS

As you imagine the end, who do you want your child to become? If you had to prioritize three to five characteristics that you hope are true for your child in the future, what would they be? Write down these characteristics. This list is your ultimate destination. It will help you navigate big decisions in the future. Share these characteristics with those you invite to your child's baby dedication. It will help them better support you and your child in the years to come.

What are three to five characteristics you hope will be true about your child in the future?

....

....

....

....

....

....

CREATE A PHYSICAL REMINDER

You may want to give a gift, like a first storybook Bible, to commemorate the moment. You may choose to plant a tree. You could take a picture, write down who came and what they said, and write a letter for your child to open on a significant birthday or at graduation. There are a hundred ways to mark the significance of this moment. The way you commemorate it is entirely up to you.

What's one way to commemorate your Baby Dedication?

....

....

....

....

....

....

Look for more ideas on Baby Dedication and how to clarify what matters on *TheParentcue.com*.

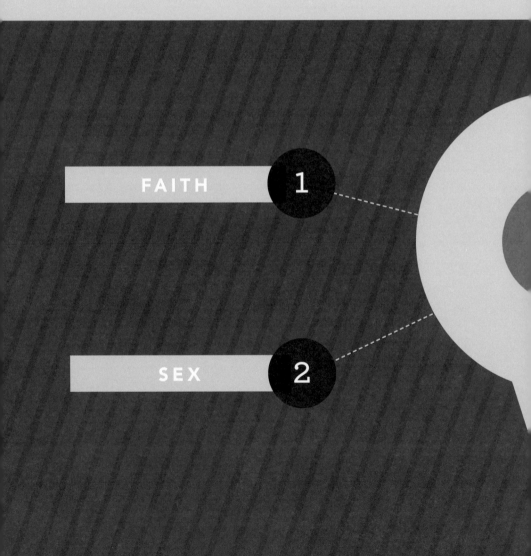

NAVI

THE CRITICAL

FAITH 1

SEX 2

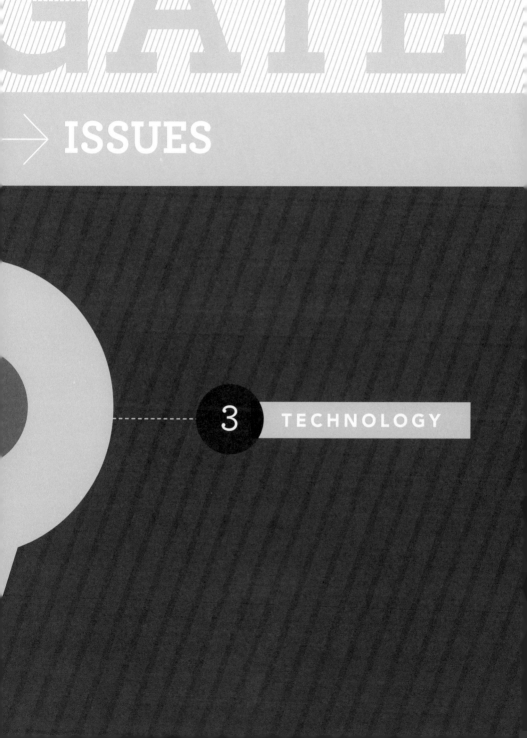

GATE

→ ISSUES

3 TECHNOLOGY

The way you parent during the next 52 weeks
will have an impact on the 884 weeks that follow.

Every phase builds on the phases that precede it
(except the Zero to One Phase when you have a fresh start).

And every phase lays a foundation for the phases that will
come after it.

In this way, the phases are all connected. That's why you
can't simply parent your baby as if they will be a baby
forever—another phase is just around the corner.

When you are faced with critical parenting issues, remember
what you know about the present realities for your baby, and
also consider what you want to be true about their future.

WEEKS

Look ahead at the weeks that are coming, and consider how you can best prepare them for the next phase.

This section explores three critical issues that are common for every phase: FAITH, SEX, and TECHNOLOGY. With each child's future in mind, we will offer suggested strategies for navigating these issues in a way that is both phase-specific and future-oriented.

SO DON'T MISS
THE **FUTURE**
IMPLICATIONS OF ...

ZERO
— TO —
ONE

IMAGINE THE END

So what are the future implications of this phase? Honestly, there are a host of things you will navigate over the next several years like regulating sugar intake, managing wardrobes, rating movies, redecorating bedrooms, maybe even refereeing sibling rivalries. We just picked Faith, Sex and Technology because after countless conversations with teachers, Starbuck managers, leaders, therapists, and parole officers, these three issues seem to keep surfacing more than most.

In the same way you will imagine the end when you prepare for a baby dedication, it's also important to imagine the end for these three critical issues. Remember, imagining the end just means you identify the end goal, then you rewind your parenting strategy and begin thinking in terms of specific steps that can be applied at every phase.

For example . . .

If you want your child to graduate from high school,
then enroll them in the first grade.

If you want your child to be healthy,
then give them vitamins.

If you want your child to win *American Idol*,
then make sure they're born with some natural talent.

This section is designed to help you "imagine the end" when it comes to Faith, Sex, and Technology. So we begin with three suggested end goals:

AUTHENTIC FAITH

Trusting Jesus in a way that transforms how I love God, myself, and the rest of the world.

SEXUAL INTEGRITY

Guarding my potential for intimacy through appropriate boundaries and mutual respect.

TECHNOLOGICAL RESPONSIBILITY

Leveraging the potential of online experiences to enhance my offline community and success.

You can customize these goals to reflect what you would like to see happen in the life of your son or daughter. What follows are phase-specific applications for parenting with these goals in mind.

one

FAITH

BY: REGGIE JOINER

IMAGINE THE END:
AUTHENTIC FAITH

Trusting Jesus in a way that transforms
how I love God, myself, and the rest of the world.

From zero to one, your baby probably won't read the Bible, pray, or do much of anything you would recognize as an attempt to know God. But don't let that fool you. What is happening in your baby's life is foundational for their spiritual development.

This is the phase where your child is learning to trust—or not to trust. When their environment is consistently warm and secure, babies feel safe and they develop trust. If their environment is characterized by hurt, neglect, or abuse, babies feel unsafe and they develop mistrust. This sense of trust or distrust extends to your baby's first impressions of their heavenly Father and the community of faith.

"Children develop a basic trust in themselves, others, and God through adults who trust themselves, other people and God."

IRIS CULLY

Think about it this way: You and your child are both created in the image of God. Maybe that's why two things will potentially happen over this first phase.

    1. You will see God in a new way.
    2. Your child will see God for the first time.

Stop and think about that for a moment. Hasn't having a child already changed the way you see God? In turn, you have the potential to impact how your child sees God. You and other key caring adults will become your child's first impression of God. That means...

IN THE ZERO TO ONE PHASE

You will
EMBRACE
their physical needs.

We've already said, when you EMBRACE your baby's physical needs, you give them an early impression of love and care so they can learn to trust. But practically, when you embrace your baby's physical needs, you also help them know God's love and meet God's family.

Stated another way, since your zero to one-year-old has no recognition of who Jesus is, your role is simple—to love them like God loves you. The first step toward authentic faith is introducing your son or daughter to people who reflect God's love. The way we have defined Authentic Faith in the beginning of this section is simply a recap of what Jesus said is the Great Commandment. Faith in Jesus ultimately expresses itself in the context of love. When you love God, it impacts how you love others and how you love yourself.

So when it comes to building authentic faith in your children, imagine that you are constantly turning three relational dials.

Wonder helps them tune-in to their relationship with God.

Discovery helps them increase the way they value others.

Passion helps them adjust how they see themselves.

What if these three dials could be turned up or down at different volumes to create a unique mix that would resonate effectively with each phase? For example, the relationship with God dial (or the WONDER dial as we call it) gets turned up a lot louder during the Zero to One Phase. It makes sense to incite WONDER in the heart of a preschooler about a heavenly Father who made them and loves them. Later, in the elementary phases you will begin turning the other two dials louder as children grow mentally and morally. But for now, giving them a tangible impression of their heavenly Father is your first priority. Why? Because if you want your child to grow up and trust God, it ultimately starts with how they trust you.

So, here are some practical ways to turn up the WONDER Dial during this phase.

ESTABLISH A RHYTHM

One of the simplest and most effective strategies for you to develop faith in your baby is to take advantage of the rhythm of your week. In the Zero to One Phase, you will already probably be establishing a routine around nap times and bath times. So it makes sense to connect faith to the everyday routine that comes with caring for your baby. Here's an idea for what those times can look like:

MORNING TIME	DRIVE TIME	BATH TIME	CUDDLE TIME
Set the mood for the day. Smile. Greet them with words of love.	Reinforce simple ideas. Talk to your baby and play music as you go.	Wind down together. Provide comfort as the day draws to a close.	Be personal. Spend one-on-one time that communicates love and affection.

You can also use these times to weave in the following faith activities:

PRAY FOR THEM WHILE YOU ARE WITH THEM

There is something unique about praying for your child while you are with them. They may not understand all of your words, but they can sense your attitude toward God and your love for them.

REPEAT CORE TRUTHS

Beyond first impressions, your baby can actually begin to grasp some fundamental faith concepts. Just remember, your baby will understand roughly seventy words by her first birthday, so she probably won't memorize many memory verses this year. Keep it simple, use repetition, and focus on what matters most. Here are three basic truths worth repeating in the Zero to One Phase:

GOD MADE ME.	GOD LOVES ME.	JESUS WANTS TO BE MY FRIEND FOREVER.

PLAY OR SING SONGS

Music is an effective tool at every phase to inspire faith and delight a child. Be sure to add some songs to your mix that remind your family and child about God's love.

* For more ideas on how to leverage time and faith activities every week, check out the Parent CUE app on Android or iPhone.

TURNING THE WONDER DIAL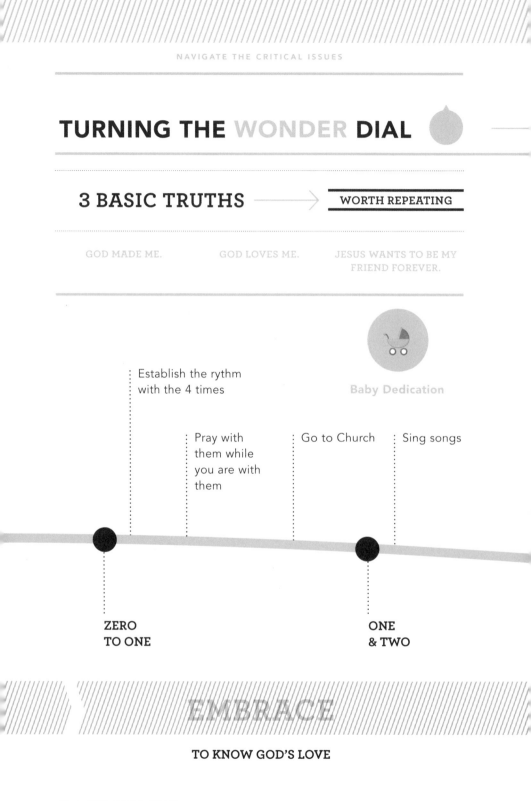

3 BASIC TRUTHS ⟶ WORTH REPEATING

GOD MADE ME.   GOD LOVES ME.   JESUS WANTS TO BE MY
FRIEND FOREVER.

Establish the rythm
with the 4 times

Baby Dedication

Pray with
them while
you are with
them

Go to Church   Sing songs

ZERO
TO ONE

ONE
& TWO

EMBRACE

TO KNOW GOD'S LOVE

TO HELP THEM KNOW GOD

4 TIMES ⟶ **TO TALK ABOUT FAITH**

MORNING TIME   DRIVE TIME   BATH TIME   CUDDLE TIME

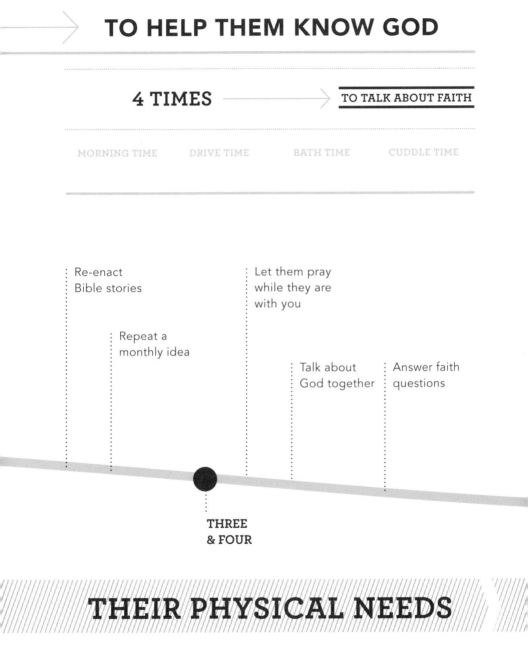

Re-enact
Bible stories

Repeat a
monthly idea

Let them pray
while they are
with you

Talk about
God together

Answer faith
questions

**THREE
& FOUR**

THEIR PHYSICAL NEEDS

TO MEET GOD'S LOVE

———— *two* ————

SEX

BY: DR. JIM BURNS

IMAGINE THE END:
SEXUAL INTEGRITY

Guarding my potential for intimacy through appropriate
boundaries and mutual respect.

If you want to raise your child to have sexual integrity one day—936
weeks from now—it begins with an understanding that we have all been
made in the image of God.

When a child believes they have been made in the image of God, and
when they see others as made in the image of God as well, it has a
profound affect on their relationships:

» It changes the way they feel about their own body.
» It changes their view of how they should treat other people.
» It changes the way they navigate their sexuality.

It may seem like it's too early to talk about things like sexuality. But in fact, research shows that having conversations with children, beginning when they are very young, delays the age at which they begin having sex and makes it less likely that they will engage in risky sexual behaviors.[45] That means parenting your child to have a healthy sexuality can't be reserved for adolescence.

Remember this is a phase characterized by:
» Rapid physical growth
» Curiosity about their body
» No inhibitions around nudity

Sexuality is a part of who we are even from the beginning. So even though you may not be having "The Talk" with your nine-month-old, you do have a role to play in navigating this critical issue.

IN THE ZERO TO ONE PHASE

You will
INTRODUCE
them to their body.

As you introduce your child to the body God made for them, you let them know their body is a good and acceptable thing. You can begin very early in life helping your child know they have been well-made because they were made by and made in the image of a good Creator. So, let's keep it simple. Here are two things you can do *now* that will help lay a foundation for the many talks to come:

START WITH THE BASICS
Tell your child: "God made you" as you change, bathe, hold, and play with them. Use specific examples: "God made your beautiful eyes. God made your strong little legs."

ASSIGN NAMES
Teach correct names for body parts. "Hoo-Hoo", "vee-vee", "winky", and "todger" are not the technical terms for body parts. If you aren't certain of the right words, try some of these: "God made your eyes. God made your elbows. God made your penis / vagina. God made your toes."

INTRODUCE THEM

**IMAGINE
THE END**

SEXUAL
INTEGRITY

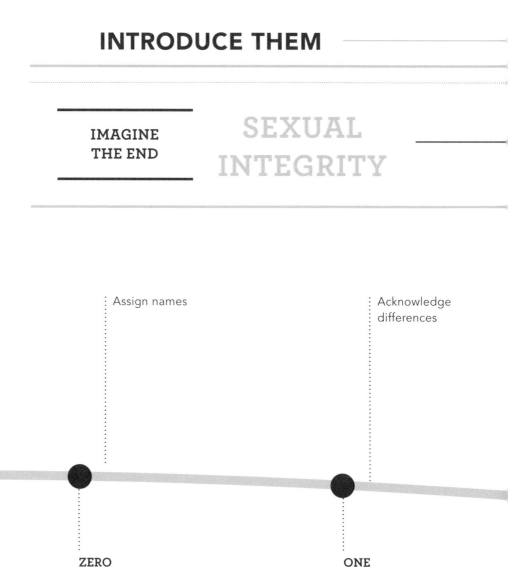

Assign names

Acknowledge
differences

**ZERO
TO ONE**

**ONE
& TWO**

TO THEIR BODY

GUARDING MY POTENTIAL FOR INTIMACY THROUGH APPROPRIATE BOUNDARIES AND MUTUAL RESPECT

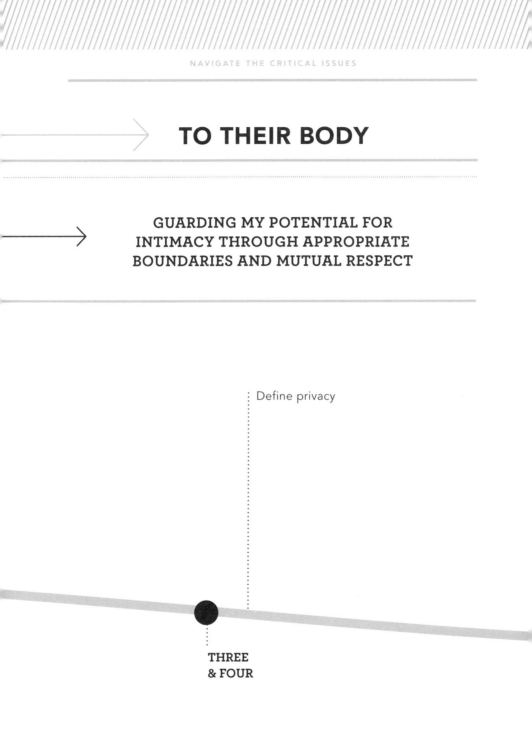

Define privacy

THREE & FOUR

three

TECHNOLOGY
BY: JON ACUFF

IMAGINE THE END:
TECHNOLOGICAL RESPONSIBILITY

Leveraging the potential of online experiences to enhance my offline community and success.

Today is the smallest social media will ever be. It only gets larger every day. That means as you parent your child, you will find yourself navigating a world of ever-changing technological opportunities. On the one hand, you can't imagine the end for technology because who can predict what gear and gadgets we'll have in five to ten years? Maybe we'll finally have hoverboards! On the other hand, you can create a goal and a strategy that will result in the kind of technological freedom that will enhance, rather than limit, your child's future.

The key to technological responsibility is the ability to see yourself and everyone else as created in the image of God.

Through that lens, technology can become a vehicle to develop your child's sense of wonder, their learning, their community, and their self image. It also increases their potential to do good and their ability to discover a purpose.

That may seem like a pretty big goal when your child can't even say the word "iPad." But before you know it, they will be pushing a button and turning on a screen. So even in this phase, you can play a role in their technological engagement.

IN THE ZERO TO ONE PHASE

You will
ENJOY
the benefits.

For now, enjoy the benefits. That may sound like the easiest goal you've had in your life—and maybe it is. Parenting a baby is hard work. But guess what? Technology has some incredible benefits for you and for your baby, when you let yourself enjoy what it has to offer. Here are a few practical ideas to help you navigate technology while they "need you now."

USE THE TOOLS . . . BUT DON'T BE USED BY THEM

Know why you'll notice that your kid's poop is a different color than normal? Because there's an app for that. With the apps and websites available, it's easy to measure every bit of data concerning your baby. If that's how you're wired, go for it! If not, don't feel like a failure. There are ways to invest in your baby's life that don't involve spreadsheets.

ENJOY THE DANCING LIGHTS . . . WITHIN REASON

Babies love technology. The warm glow of a screen will draw them like a moth to a flame. More than likely, you will at some point sit your baby down for a minute with the TV or the iPad. Enjoy the "in a pinch" babysitter that technology can be, but keep an eye on how much their eyes are engaged with technology. They'll never tell you it's too much.

REMEMBER YOU'RE NOT ALONE

This year you'll probably go out less, talk to adults less, and feel more isolated than you have in the past. But you aren't alone. There's a rich community of moms and dads online just like you. We live in the most connected age mankind has ever known, so you don't have to do the Zero to One Phase by yourself.

ENJOY THE BENEFITS

**IMAGINE
THE END**

TECHNOLOGICAL RESPONSIBILITY

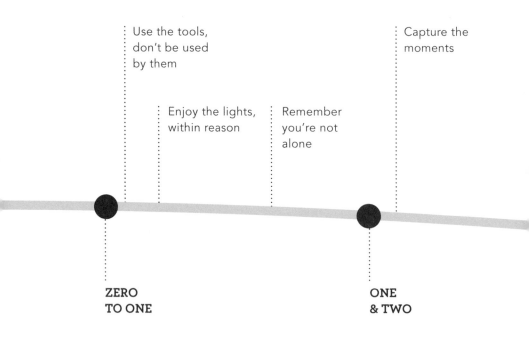

Use the tools,
don't be used
by them

Capture the
moments

Enjoy the lights,
within reason

Remember
you're not
alone

**ZERO
TO ONE**

**ONE
& TWO**

OF TECHNOLOGY

LEVERAGING THE POTENTIAL OF ONLINE EXPERIENCES TO ENHANCE MY OFFLINE COMMUNITY AND SUCCESS

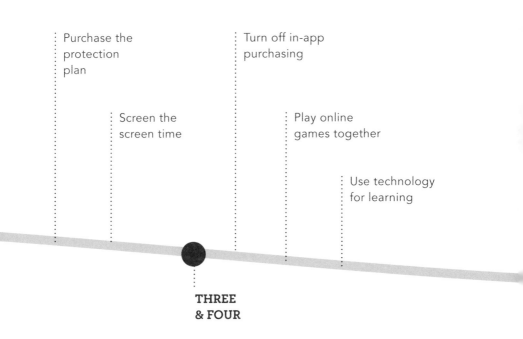

Purchase the protection plan

Turn off in-app purchasing

Screen the screen time

Play online games together

Use technology for learning

THREE & FOUR

WHAT'S COMING UP

ONE OF THE JOYS OF PARENTING IS THE MANY SURPRISES THAT GREET YOU AROUND EVERY CORNER.

WE CAN'T PREPARE YOU FOR ALL THE JOYS THAT AWAIT YOU IN THE NEXT PHASE, BUT WE CAN GIVE YOU A GLIMPSE OF A FEW THINGS THAT MIGHT HELP YOU ANTICIPATE WHAT'S COMING.

» DISCIPLINE

» CHOOSING A PRESCHOOL

» FORGETTING THE DIAPER BAG WHEN YOUR TODDLER HAS A "BLOW OUT"

» TEETHING

» CALLING YOUR CHILD BY THE PET'S NAME

» GRADUATING FROM THE CRIB TO A "BIG BED"

» UNPLUGGING THE BABY MONITOR . . . MAYBE

» YOUR CHILD SAYING A WORD YOU DIDN'T KNOW THEY OVERHEARD

» A TOTAL LOSS OF PERSONAL BATHROOM PRIVACY

» PULLING SOMETHING OUT OF YOUR TODDLER'S MOUTH AND PUTTING IT BACK INTO THE TRASH

» WATCHING YOUR TODDLER LICK A "DISGUSTING" SURFACE

» ART . . . MADE WITH OR ON SOMETHING UNEXPECTED

» TEMPER TANTRUMS

» YOUR CHILD FEEDING THEMSELF—WITHOUT YOUR HELP

» WATCHING YOUR CHILD CLIMB STAIRS

» CHILD-PROOFING THE HOUSE

» GETTING TICKLED BACK

NEXT

IN ONLY

52
W E E K S

THE

"I NEED YOU NOW"

PHASE WILL BEGIN TO FADE INTO THE PAST.

YOU WILL BEGIN TO DISCOVER A NEW PHASE WITH A WHOLE NEW SET OF

PRESENT REALITIES

DISTINCTIVE OPPORTUNITIES

AND

FUTURE IMPLICATIONS

SO, MAKE THE MOST OF THIS PRESENT PHASE BECAUSE BEFORE YOU KNOW IT, YOU WILL FIND YOURSELF FACING A NEW PHASE.

IN NOT SO MANY WEEKS YOU MAY DISCOVER YOU ARE LIVING WITH AN EMERGING TODDLER WHO IS READY TO SHOW YOU

"I CAN DO IT."

ONE
AND TWO

THE PHASE WHEN NOBODY'S ON TIME,
EVERYTHING'S A MESS, AND ONE
EAGER TODDLER WILL INSIST,
"I CAN DO IT."

EXPECT TO BE LATE DURING THIS PHASE.

Maybe you had to wait for your toddler to "do it myself" (just try and stop them). Or maybe they impressively filled a clean diaper just as you got into the car. Whatever the reason, this phase will make even the most punctual adult miss the mark occasionally.

YOU CAN ALSO LOOK FORWARD TO A FEW FASHION STATEMENTS.

Expect a few mismatched outfits, magic marker tattoos, sticker collages, and other various states of creative expression. In this phase, you will choose not only your battles, but also which messes will just have to be tolerated.

THE GREATEST TENSION OF THIS PHASE CAN BE SUMMED UP IN THE PHRASE "I CAN DO IT."

Their struggle for independence has begun. You feel it the first time they try to feed themselves and dump applesauce down the front of their shirt. Just remember, they're not only learning new skills, they're also developing the confidence they need in order to move on to the next phase.

IT'S JUST A PHASE   (L)   SO DON'T MISS IT

OTHER RESOURCES

TO UNDERSTAND MORE ABOUT THE PRESCHOOL PHASE:

BabyCenter.com

Brain Rules for Baby: How to Raise a Smart and Happy Child from Zero to Five by John Medina (Pear Press, 2014)

The Emotional Life of the Toddler by Alicia F. Lieberman (Free Press, 1995)

How to Raise a Child with a High EQ: A Parents' Guide to Emotional Intelligence by Lawrence Shapiro (Harper Perennial, 1998)

Mind in the Making: The Seven Essential Life Skills Every Child Neds by Ellen Galinsky (William Morrow Paperbacks, 2010)

Momtastic.com

Momsoncall.com

Parents.com

Pbs.org/parents

Personality Plus for Parents: Understanding What Makes Your Child Tick by Florence Littauer (Revell, 2000)

Scholastic.com/parents

The Wonder Weeks: How to Stimulate Your Baby's Mental Development and Help Him Turn His 10 Predictable, Great, Fussy Phases into Magical Leaps by Rijt Hetty and Frans X. Plooij (Kiddy World Publishing; Updated edition, 2013)

The Wonder Years by American Acaemy of Pediatrics (Bantam Books, 2007)

Touchpoints – Birth to Three by T. Berry Brazelton, M.D Joshua D. Sparrow, M.D (Da Capo Press; Second Edition, 2006)

What's Going on in There?: How the Brain and Mind Develop in the First Five Years by Lisa Elliot (Random House Publishing Group, 2000)

WholesomeBabyFood.com

Your Child's Growing Mind: Brain Development and Learning From Birth to Adolescence by Jane Healy (Harmony, 2004)

ZerotoThree.org

TO HELP YOU LEVERAGE THE PRESCHOOL PHASE:

Gymboree 365 Activities You and Your Baby Will Love by Roni Leiderman and Wendy Masi

Blessings of a Skinned Knee: Using Jewish Teachings to Raise Self-Reliant Children by Wendy Mogel (Scribner, 2008)

Games to Play with Two-Year-Old by Jackie Silberg (Gryphon House; Revised Edition (May 1, 2002)

Happier at Home: Kiss More, Jump More, Abandon Self-Control, and My Other Experiments in Everyday Life by Gretchen Rubin (Harmony, 2013)

Legacy Marble App (for Android and iPhone)

MoneyAsYouGrow.org

Parenting is Wonderful by Sue Miller and Holly Delich (Orange. 2014)

Parent Cue App (for Android and iPhone)

Playful Parenting: A Bold New Way to Nurture Close Connections, Solve Behavior Problems, and Encourage Children's Confidence by Lawrence Cohen (Ballantine, 2001)

Playing for Keeps: 6 Things Every Kid Needs by Reggie Joiner and Kristen Ivy (Orange, 2013)

Positive Discipline by Jane Nelsen Ed.D. (Ballantine Books; Updated edition, 2006)

Raising Your Spirited Child: A Guide for Parents Whose Child Is More Intense, Sensitive, Perceptive, Persistent, Energetic by Mary Sheedy Kurcinka (Harper, 2006)

TheParentCue.org

TO HELP YOU CELEBRATE THE PRESCHOOL PHASE:

Celebrations.com

Family Fun Magazine

Parents.com/holiday

TO HELP YOU NAVIGATE THE PRESCHOOL PHASE:

Joining Children on the Spiritual Journey by Catherine Stonehouse (Bridgepoint Books, 1998)

Teaching Your Children Healthy Sexuality by Jim Burns (Pure Foundations, 2008)

Simple Truths: A Simple, Natural Approach to Discussing Sex With Your Children by Mary Flo Ridley (Just Say Yes, 2009)

AUTHORS

REGGIE JOINER

Reggie Joiner, founder and CEO of the reThink Group, has journeyed through the phases with four kids of his own. He and his wife Debbie raised Reggie Paul (RP), Hannah, Sarah and Rebekah, and now they're well into the phases not covered in this book.

The rethink Group (also known as Orange) is a non-profit organization whose purpose is to influence those who influence the next generation. Orange provides resources and training for churches and organizations that create environments for parents, kids, and teenagers.

Before founding the reThink Group in 2006, Reggie was one of the founders of North Point Community Church. During his 11 years with Andy Stanley, Reggie was the executive director of family ministry where he developed a new concept for relevant ministry for children, teenagers, and married adults.

Reggie has authored and co-authored ten books including: *Think Orange, Seven Practices of Effective Ministry, Parenting Beyond Your Capacity, Playing for Keeps, Lead Small, Creating a Lead Small Culture,* and his latest *It's Just a Phase So Don't Miss It.*

For more about Reggie, visit ReggieJoiner.com or connect with him on Twitter @ReggieJoiner.

KRISTEN IVY

Kristen Ivy, executive director of messaging at Orange, and her husband Matt are in the middle of the preschool phase with a Kindergartener (Sawyer), a preschooler (Hensley), and her own "Zero to One" baby (Raleigh).

Before beginning her career at reThink in 2006, Kristen earned her Bachelors of Education from Baylor University in 2004 and a Master of Divinity from Mercer University in 2009. She worked in the public school as a high school Biology and English teacher, where she learned firsthand the importance of influencing the next generation.

At Orange, Kristen has played an integral role in the development of the elementary, middle school, and high school curriculums and has shared her experiences at speaking events across the country. Kristen is a co-author of *Playing for Keeps*, *Creating a Lead Small Culture*, and *It's Just a Phase So Don't Miss It*.

You can follow Kristen's work on the Phase project at *JustAPhase.com*, or connect with her on Twitter @Kristen_Ivy.

FOREWARD
HOLLY CRAWSHAW

Holly is a wife, mother, and writer who eats sour candy and laughs at her own jokes. While in college, she helped found a ministry for middle and high school students. After graduation, she worked as a high school English teacher, then served on staff with North Point Ministries for six years, including part of that time as Preschool Director. She currently consults and writes curriculum for the preschool curriculum at Orange. She and her husband Ben are raising their two daughters, Lilah and Esmae, in their hometown of Cumming, Georgia.

SEXUALITY
JIM BURNS

Jim Burns is president of HomeWord and executive director of the HomeWord Center for Youth and Family at Azusa Pacific University. Jim speaks to thousands of people around the world each year. He has over 1.5 million resources in print in over 25 languages. Jim's radio broadcast is heard on over 800 stations a day and heard around the world via podcast at *HomeWord.com*. Some of his books include *Faith Conversations for Families, Confident Parenting, The Purity Code* and *Creating an Intimate Marriage*. Jim and his wife, Cathy and their three daughters live in Southern California.

TECHNOLOGY
JON ACUFF

Jon Acuff is the New York Times Bestselling author of five books including his most recent, *Do Over: Rescue Monday, Reinvent Your Work and Never Get Stuck*. For 17 years he's helped some of the biggest brands in the world tell their story. He's written for *Fast Company, the Harvard Business Review, CNBC* and many other national media outlets. In 2010 he used his influence with his tribe to build two kindergartens in Vietnam. Jon lives with his wife Jenny and two daughters, L.E. and McRae, in Franklin, Tennessee. You can read more of his work at *Acuff.me* or on Twitter @JonAcuff.

CONTRIBUTORS

RESEARCH AND DEVELOPMENT TEAM

Sarah Anderson
Sara Bragg
Elle Campbell
Elizabeth Higgins
Crystal Chiang
Holly Crawshaw
Kathy Hill
Mike Jeffries
Darren Kizer
Brooklyn Lindsey
Cara Martens
Nina Schmidgall
Dan Scott
Deb Springer
Lauren Terrell
Melanie Williams
Karen Wilson

PROFESSIONAL ADVISORS

Sharai Bradshaw M.A.
Lydia Criss Mays Ph.D.
Jackie Dunagan LMFT
Mallory Even LPMT, MT-BC
Laura Lenz MT-BC
Nicole Manry Ph.D.
Debra McDonald, Ohio Teacher of the Year, 2014
Laura Meyers Ph.D.
Hannah Rinehart M.A., LPC, NCC
Deborah Smith M.A., LPC
Chinwé Williams Ph.D., LPC, NCC, CPCS
Jenifer Wilmoth LMFT

CREATIVE CONTRIBUTORS

Anna Aigner-Muhler
Frank Bealer
Jessica Bealer
Abby Carr
Mike Clear
Sam Collier
Ben Crawshaw
Alexa Felice
Amy Fenton
Pam Haight
Elizabeth Hansen
Donny Joiner
Kacey Lanier
Paul Montaperto
Lindsey Needham
Ben Nunes
Brandon O'Dell
Greg Payne
Kevin Ragsdale
Grace Segars
Angie Smith
Melissa Thorson
Colette Taylor
Autumn Ward
Jon Williams

ENDNOTES

1   Tynan, Dan, and Christina Wood. "Your Amazing Baby: 'Wow!'-Worthy Development Facts." *Babycenter.com.* http://www.babycenter.com /0_your-amazing-baby-wow-worthy-development- facts_10386124.bc.

2   "Growth Charts." *CDC.gov.* Last modified September 9, 2010. http:// www.cdc.gov/growthcharts/who_charts.htm.

3   DeCasper, AJ, and WP Fifer. "Of Human Bonding: Newborns Prefer Their Mothers' Voices." *Science Magazine,* June 6, 1980, 1174-76. doi:10.1126/science.7375928.

4   "Infant Brain Stimulation." *Huggamind.com.* http://huggamind.com /highcontrast.php.

5   Batki, Anna, Simon Baron-Cohen, Sally Wheelwright, Jennifer Connellan, and Jag Ahluwalia. "Is There an Innate Gaze Module? Evidence from Human Neonates." Abstract. Infant Behavior and Development 23, no. 2 (February 2000). doi:10.1016/S0163-6383(01)00037-6..; Turati, Chiara, Francesca Simion, Idana Milani, and Carlo Umilta. "Newborns' Preference for Faces: What Is Crucial?" *Developmental Psychology* 38, no. 6 (November 2002): 875-82.

6   Farroni, Teresa, Gergely Csibra, Francesca Simeon, and Mark H. Johnson. "Eye Contact Detection in Humans From Birth." *PNAS* 99, no. 14 (July 9, 2002). doi:10.1073/pnas.152159999.

7   Bushneil, W.R., F. Sai, and J.T. Mulllin. "Neonatal recognition of the mother's face." *British Journal of Developmental Psychology* 7, no. 1 (March 1989): 3-15. doi:10.1111/j.2044-835X.1989.tb00784.x.

8   Graham, Judith. "Children and Brain Development: What We Know about How Children Learn." Edited by Leslie A. Forstadt. *University of Maine.* Last modified 2011. http://umaine.edu/publications/4356e/.

9 Ibid.

10 Morris, Desmond. *Amazing Baby: The Amazing Story of the First Two Years of Life.* N.p.: Firefly Books, 2008.

11 Gopnick, Alison. *The Philosophical Baby: What Children's Minds Tell Us About Truth, Love, and the Meaning of Life.* New York, NY: Farrar, Straus and Giroux, 2009.

12 Healy, Jane M. *Your Child's Growing Mind: Brain Development and Learning From Birth to Adolescence.* 3rd ed. N.p.: Harmony, 2004.

13 Eliot, Lise. *What's Going on in There? : How the Brain and Mind Develop in the First Five Years of Life.* N.p.: Bantam, 2000.

14 Konner, Melvin. *The Evolution of Childhood: Relationships, Emotion, Mind.* N.p.: Belknap Press, 2011.

15 Gopnick, *Philosophical Baby.*

16 Konner, Melvin. *The Evolution of Childhood: Relationships, Emotion, Mind.* N.p.: Belknap Press, 2011.

17 "When will my baby know her name?" *Parents.com.* http://www.parents.com/advice/babies/baby-development/when-will-my-baby-know-her-name/

18 *The Laughing Stork.* Last modified 2014. http://thelaughingstork.com.

19 Cryer, Debby, Thelma Harms, and Beth Bourland. *Active Learning for Infants.* Addison-Wesley Active Learning. N.p.: Dale Seymour Publications, 1987.

20 Jennings, Heather. "EmotionalDevelopment" http://www.mccc.edu/~jenningh/Courses/documents/Module4-emotionaldevelopment.ppt.

21 BabyCenter Medical Advisory Board, ed. "Separation Anxiety." *BabyCenter.com* http://www.babycenter.com/0_separation-anxiety_145.bc.

22 "Diapers and Your Baby's First Year." *Kidsgrowth.com*. Last modified 2015. http://www.kidsgrowth.com/resources/articledetail.cfm?id=431.

23 *Funfactz.com*. http://www.funfactz.com/interesting-facts/new-baby -usually-deprives-each-of-its-1895.html.

24 Charlesworth, Rosalind. *Understanding Child Development: For Adults Who Work With Young Children*. 3rd ed. Albany, NY: Delmar Publishers Inc., 1992, 125.

25 Ibid.,111.

26 Tynan, Dan, and Christina Wood. "Your Amazing Baby: 'Wow!'-Worthy Development Facts."

27 Morris, Desmond. *Amazing Baby*. Buffalo, NY: Firefly Books, 2008.

28 Ibid.

29 Izard, C.E., and B.P. Ackerman. "Motivational, Organizational, and Regulatory Functions of Discrete Emotions." In *Handbook of Emotions,* by Michael Lewis and Jeannette M. Haviland-Jones. 2nd ed. New York: Guilford Press, 2000.

30 Kail, Robert. *Human Development: A Life-Span View*. Boston, MA: Cengage Learning, Jan 1, 2015

31 Beck, Laura E. "Emotional and Social Development in Infant and Toddlerhood." *Exploring Lifespan Development"*, Pearson, 2013, p 141-142.

32 Jennings, "Emotional Development."

33 Gopnik, *Philosophical Baby*.

34 Charlesworth, *Understanding Child Development*, 114.

35 Medina, John. *Brain Rules for Baby: How to Raise a Smart and Happy Child from Zero to Five.* Seattle, WA: Pear Press, 2014.

36 Bloom, Paul. "The Moral Life of Babies." *The New York Times,* May 5, 2010. http://www.nytimes.com/2010/05/09/magazine/09babies-t .html?pagewanted=all&_r=2&.

37 Ibid.

38 "Surprising Facts About Your Baby's Brain." *whattoexpect.com.* Last modified December 12, 2014. http://www.whattoexpect.com/first -year/photo-gallery/surprising-facts-about-babys-brain.aspx#/slide -3.;Gerhardt, Sue. *Why Love Matters: How Affection Shapes a Baby's Brain.* 2nd ed. N.p.: Routledge, 2014.

39 Nixon, Robin. "11 Facts Every Parent Should Know About Their Baby's Brain." *livescience.com.* Last modified February 20, 2011.http://www .livescience.com/12932-11-facts-parent-baby-brain.html.

40 For more instruction on how to use baby sign language, check out *Baby Signing* by Nancy Cadjan

41 Eliot, "What's Going on," 372.

42 Narayan, Shoba. "Encourage Your Child to Play Alone." *parents.com.* http://www.parents.com/toddlers-preschoolers/development /friendship/playing-alone/.

43 Nixon, "11 facts."

44 Ibid.

45 American Academy of Pediatrics. "Sexuality Education for Children and Adolescents." *Pediatrics* 108, no. 2 (August 1, 2001): 498-502. http:// pediatrics.aappublications.org/content/108/2/498

LOOK FOR NEW PHASE PARENTING RESOURCES AVAILABLE SOON

www.JUSTAPHASE.com